A TREATISE

ON

MARTIAL LAW,

AND

COURTS-MARTIAL;

AS PRACTISED IN THE

UNITED STATES OF AMERICA.

PUBLISHED BY ORDER OF THE UNITED STATES
MILITARY PHILOSOPHICAL SOCIETY.

BY ALEXANDER MACOMB, Esq.
*Major in the United States Corps of Engineers, late
Judge-Advocate on several Special Trials,*
M.U S.M.P.S. &c. &c.

THE LAWBOOK EXCHANGE, LTD.
Clark, New Jersey
2006

ISBN-13: 978-1-58477-709-0
ISBN-10: 1-58477-709-5

The quality of this reprint is equivalent to the quality of the original work.

Printed in the United States of America on acid-free paper

THE LAWBOOK EXCHANGE, LTD.
33 Terminal Avenue
Clark, New Jersey 07066-1321

Please see our website for a selection of our other publications and fine facsimile reprints of classic works of legal history:
www.lawbookexchange.com

Library of Congress Cataloging-in-Publication Data

Macomb, Alexander, 1782-1841.
A treatise on martial law and courts-martial : as practised in the United States of America / by Alexander Macomb.
p. cm.
Orginally published, by order of the United States Military Philosophical Society: Charleston, SC : J. Hoff, 1809.
Includes bibliographical references and index.
ISBN-13: 978-1-58477-709-0 (alk. paper)
ISBN-10: 1-58477-709-5 (alk. paper)
1. Courts-martial and courts of inquiry--United States.
I. United States Military Philosophical Society. II. Title.
KF7625.M33 2005
343.73'0143--dc22 2006005099

A TREATISE

ON

MARTIAL LAW,

AND

COURTS-MARTIAL;

AS PRACTISED IN THE

UNITED STATES OF AMERICA.

PUBLISHED BY ORDER OF THE UNITED STATES MILITARY PHILOSOPHICAL SOCIETY.

BY ALEXANDER MACOMB, Esq.
Major in the United States Corps of Engineers, late Judge-Advocate on several Special Trials,
M.U S.M.P.S. &c. &c.

CHARLESTON, (s c.)

PRINTED AND PUBLISHED, FOR THE AUTHOR, BY J. HOFF, NO. 6, BROAD-STREET.

1809.

TABLE OF CONTENTS.

CHAPTER IV.

CHAPTER V.

CHAPTER VI.

CHAPTER VII.

CHAPTER VIII.

CHAPTER IX.

APPENDIX.

PREFACE.

The following Treatise is principally compiled from the very excellent Essay on Military Law, by the Honorable Alexander Fraser Tytler, formerly Judge-Advocate of North Britain, published in 1800; and from the Author's practice and experience in Courts-Martial, with the Army on the Western Waters, and in the Atlantic States.

Nothing but the want of a Work adapted to the Martial Codes, and to the usages and forms of Courts-Martial, as practised in the United States, has induced the Author to attempt any thing of the kind; more particularly, since the subject of Military Law in general, has been so fully and amply treated on by Mr. Tytler, in his Essay above-mentioned: but as it applies principally to the Martial Laws of Great-Britain, it was thought that a revision of it, suited to our own Laws, would not be unacceptable to the Officers of the American Army, to whom it is of importance to be well acquainted not only with the forms and procedure in the trial of Crimes by Courts-Martial, but with the general doctrines of the Law of Evidence, which apply equally to the cognizance of crimes before a Military as before a Civil tribunal.

The Author claims no other merit in this work, than the trouble he has taken to suit it to the practices and Laws of our own Courts. And it would not only be ungenerous, but highly ungrateful in him as a Military man, not to acknowledge how much we are indebted to Mr. Tytler, for the pains and labor he has taken in forming so complete and correct a Treatise on the subject.

A TREATISE

ON

MARTIAL LAW,

AND

COURTS-MARTIAL.

CHAPTER I.

Of the Authority of Courts-Martial.

MARTIAL LAW, as it exists in this country, forms part of the Laws of the Land; and it is enacted by the same authority which is the origin of all other statutary regulations, and consequently has the same positive obligation on those whom it is intended to bind, as the Common and Statute Law has on all the citizens of the United States. CHAP. I.

Congress have enacted Rules and Articles for the government of the Armies of the United States, which together with the Act, fixing the Military

CHAP. I.

Peace Establishment, form, *at present*, the whole code of the Law Martial.

It follows from the terms of these Acts, that no offences or crimes against which any provision is expressly made in the Articles of War, shall be subject to any other punishment than that which is therein specified; nor shall it be in the power of any other courts or judges, to assume to themselves a right of cognizance of any of those offences properly military, and punishable only by a military tribunal.

Authority for holding Courts-Martial.

All General Courts-Martial are assembled by the authority of the President of the United States of America, or "any general officer commanding an army, or colonel commanding a separate department."*

With the appointment or constitution of the Court-Martial, the authority of the officer ordering the court ceases, until that court shall have pronounced its judgment. The President of the United States, or General, can no more

* Vide 65th Article of War.

interfere with the procedure of Courts-Martial, in the execution of their duty, than they can with any of the fixed courts of Justice; or even after the Court-Martial has pronounced its sentence is it in the power of the President, General, or other officer ordering the court, to add to or alter that sentence in any one particular, unless a recommendation to that effect shall be therein contained. The President or Commander in Chief, in virtue of his prerogative of mercy, may entirely remit the punishment, which the court has awarded, or by disapproving the sentence, he may order the court to set again, and to review their proceedings and judgment; but he can no more decree any particular alteration of their sentence, than he can alter the judgment of a civil court, or the verdict of a jury. The power of remitting the sentence of a Court-Martial again to the same court for their review, is founded on this principle; that the sentence itself is not complete, until it shall receive the sanction of the person

CHAP. I.

authorised to approve the same, and to enforce its execution.

Although the sentence of a General Court-Martial is not alterable by any person having authority to assemble Courts-Martial, yet it is at all times competent to that officer, and entirely consistent with his authority, to remark on whatever may have been either omitted by the court, or improperly judged by them; and which from its blameable nature, calls for animadversion Such remarks on the proceedings of Courts-Martial have the best effect in stimulating the care and diligence, as well as guarding the propriety and rectitude of those tribunals.

Number of members of a General Court-Martial.

It is enacted by the 64th Article of War, that "General Courts-Martial may "consist of any number of commissioned officers from five to thirteen inclusively, but they shall not consist of "less than thirteen, where that number "can be convened without manifest injury to the service."

It is in most cases proper that there should be more members nominated than the *minimum* required by Law, to guard against the accident of members falling sick, or dying, or being disqualified, and therefore it would be well to appoint one or two members more, who might be sworn with the other members, and hear all the evidence adduced, and every other circumstance relating to the trial; so that in case any member of the court should die, or of necessity be absent, either on account of an objection, or other disqualification, the court might proceed on with the matter before them, in the same manner as if no accident had happened; but it is understood that no members over and above the number of thirteen are to give any vote or opinion in passing the sentence; and the supernumerary members must always be of the inferior degree of rank among those appointed to compose the court; for it is not competent for a Court-Martial to continue its proceedings, unless all the members appointed to form the court be present; and in case any member should be disqualified by an objection or otherwise, or any circumstance should prevent the further attendance of a member, the seat so vacated must be supplied by proper authority, before the court can proceed with the matter before it. The whole of the evidence touching the case in hearing must be read over to the new member, and he may cross-examine and question the witnesses who have given their testimony, so as to elucidate such parts thereof as he may not perfectly comprehend.*

In cases where it should be thought proper and necessary to have as full a court as the situation and circumstances of the place where the court is ordered to be convened would admit, and the greatest number of officers that could be conveniently assembled would not amount to thirteen, but say only to ten

* There have been some instances in which Courts-Martial have proceeded after an objection against a member has been admitted, without the seat of the disqualified member being supplied; but in every such case the proceedings have been disapproved by the Commander in Chief, and the members severely censured.

CHAP. I

or any even number, and should they in that case be formed into a court, and in giving their opinions, be equally divided, the point ought to be considered, as decided in favor of the prisoner.

The members of a Court-Martial.

With respect to the members of a Court-Martial, as the provisions of the Rules and Articles of War extend, both to the land forces and marines, so it is declared by article 68th, that "Whenever it may be found convenient and "necessary to the public service, the "officers of the marine shall be associated with the officers of the land forces, for the purpose of holding courts-martial, and trying offenders belonging to either," and that the members so composed, shall take their rank according to the seniority of their commissions, in either service.

A General Court-Martial is, as before observed, held either by direct authority from the President of the United States, or by the authority of some officer, commanding in chief, having powers to that effect. Sometimes the orders for assembling the court contain the names of all the members, who are to compose it; and in this case it is generally addressed to the Judge-Advocate and President thereof; but it frequently happens that the President alone is appointed by name, and the other members to be taken by *Roster* from the different regiments and of a certain rank; this detail is usually left with the Adjutant General, or officer acting as such.

The court exists till it is dissolved.

The court-martial once constituted by proper authority, remains in existence until it is dissolved by the same authority which created it. The members, therefore, though the whole business is exhausted by their pronouncing sentence on the trials before them, are not at liberty to return to their ordinary duty, or leave the place where the court is assembled, without special permission, till the court is finally dissolved. It may be necessary for the court to revise its sentence, or they may be required to intimate the pleasure of the President of the United States thereon, or that of the Commander in Chief, to the parties in open court.

The court must discuss the whole of the Charges.

A Court-Martial must exhaust the whole charges that come before them, either by separate opinions and judgments upon each separate article, or where the several charges are connected and form altogether one offence, by a sentence referring to the whole. It is not competent for the court, after taking cognizance of one or more of the articles of charge, and pronouncing sentence thereon, even though that sentence should award the *ultimum supplicium*, death, to wave, on that account, the discussion of other articles of charge that may remain. Because it is of importance to the public, that every thing which has been made a matter of criminal accusation, should undergo a solemn decision by the proper tribunal, that it may have effectual operation in guarding others from falling into similar practices.

The necessity of examining and discussing the whole of the articles of charge, which are brought before a

CHAP. I.

Court-Martial, does not preclude their exercise of judgment on the irrelevancy of those charges, or on their competency to become the subject of trial. It frequently happens, when charges are exhibited by a private prosecutor, involving the consideration of various articles of alledged misconduct or malversation, that the prosecutor, either from over anxiety or error in judgment, specifies certain matters as articles of charge, which a court may judge to be of a nature entirely blameless; and that although proved, or acknowledged by the prisoner, they infer no criminality. In such a case it is the duty of the court to dismiss the charge altogether, and throw it out of their consideration as *irrelevant*. In like manner, where a charge appears, either from self-evident circumstances, or from facts emerging in the course of the trial, not to attach upon the party accused, it is the duty of the court to wave all examination into the subject, as being foreign to the person of the prisoner, and to be declared so by their sentence.

CHAP. I.

Precedence among the members of the court.

The members both of General and Regimental Courts-Martial, when belonging to different corps, take the same rank which they hold in the army; officers of equal grade take place according to the dates of their commissions. But as it sometimes happens that officers have commissions of the same degree and date, then and in that case an inspection must be had into their former commissions:—for instance, if two lieutenants are promoted on the same day to the rank of captain, he who took rank as elder lieutenant will of course take precedence as captain; but if it should so happen that their lieutenants' commissions are of the same date, their ensigns' commissions, or other previous service must be taken in like manner into consideration, and then length of service must determine the place which each officer is to hold in the court. It is enacted, article 61st of the Rules and Articles of War, that "Officers having brevets or "commissions of a prior date to those "of the regiments in which they serve, "may take place in courts-martial, and

CHAP. I.

"on detachment when composed of different corps, according to the ranks given them in their brevets or dates of their former commissions; but in the regiment, troop, or company, to which such officers belong, they shall do duty, and take rank, both in Courts-Martial and on detachments, which shall be composed of their own corps, according to the commissions by which they are mustered in the said corps." And it is also enacted by article 98th, that "All officers, serving by commission from the authority of any particular State, shall on all detachments, Courts-Martial, or other duty, wherein they may be employed in conjunction with the regular forces of the United States, take rank, next after all officers of the like grade in the said regular forces, notwithstanding the commissions of such militia or state officers may be elder than the commissions of the officers of the regular forces of the United States."

Time of setting.

Courts-Martial are not by law allowed to sit longer than seven hours a-day; and no court can be assembled before eight o'clock in the morning, or sit later than three o'clock in the afternoon, unless in cases which require an immediate example.*

Those who are subject to Military Law.

The persons who are subject to Military Law, and amenable to be tried by Courts-Martial, are all persons who are commissioned or in pay as officers, or who are enlisted or in pay as non-commissioned officers or soldiers, "All sut-" "lers and retainers to the camp, and all" "persons whatsoever serving with the" "armies of the United States in the" "field though not enlisted soldiers,"† all military storekeepers, commissaries, military agents, assistant military agents, surgeons, surgeons' mates, paymasters, quarter-masters, chaplains, "all" "officers, conductors, gunners, matros-" "ses, drivers, or other persons, whatso-" "ever, receiving pay or hire, in the ser-" "vice of the Artillery or Corps of Engi-" "neers of the United States,"‡ and all

* Article of War 75. † Article of War 60.
‡ Article of War 96.

CHAP. I.

Militia subject to Martial Law when acting with the regular forces.

officers and soldiers of any other troops, whether militia, or others, being mustered and in pay of the United States, when acting in conjunction with the regular forces, but the militia are liable to be tried by Courts-Martial composed of militia officers only.*

It had formerly been a matter of doubt in the British service, whether an officer or soldier after being dismissed, or discharged from the service, could be brought to trial before a Court-Martial, for a crime committed while he was in commission or in pay; as the operation of the military law appeared to be confined to those who are actually in commission or in pay. The point came solemnly to be determined in the case of Lord George Sackville, who immediately on his return to England after the battle of Minden, had been deprived by the king of Great-Britain of all military command and commission, but was not brought to trial for his conduct in that engagement until some

* Articles of War 97.

months afterwards, in consequence of his own demand of a Court Martial. The question was referred to the opinion of the twelve Judges, who by their answer, unanimously declared, that "They saw no ground to doubt the "legality of the jurisdiction of a Court-"Martial in those circumstances."*

It has likewise been made a matter of doubt in the American army, whether an officer who is under a suspension from service for a limited time, and who shall in that interval commit any crime or offence in breach of the Rules and Articles of War, be subject to military law, and amenable to a Court-Martial for his conduct: but this doubt may easily be solved on a moments reflection. Suspension, though it has the effect of depriving an officer for the time of his rank and pay, and putting a stop to the ordinary discharge of his military duties, does not void his commission, annihilate the military character, or dissolve that connection, which subsists

* Third of March, 1760.

CHAP. I.

between him and the government in whose service he may be: he retains his commission, and is at all times liable to a call to duty, which would take off the sentence. Suspension being a punishment, is regulated in its effects by the tenor of the sentence which inflicts it, and which, as it bears no more than the temporary deprivation of rank and pay, must be limited in its consequences to those effects alone, leaving every other particular of the military character entire. The suspended officer remains, therefore, subject to the military law, and is punishable for every breach thereof committed during his suspension.

The advantages of trial by Courts-Martial.

The mode of trial by Courts-Martial possesses all the benefit of trial by jury, and has moreover many advantages that are peculiar to itself. It has been frivolously urged, that the essence of the trial by "his peers or equals," non-commissioned officers and private soldiers, when tried by a Court-Martial, have not that benefit, as the Articles of War declare, that no member shall be under the degree of a commissioned officer. But in truth, this objection is founded entirely in a misunderstanding of the meaning of the words "*trial by peers.*" By this expression it is not meant that the persons who compose the court should be, in every respect, of the same rank and station in life with the party who is to be tried, for this would in some cases be an unattainable requisite, and in many would be attended with much disadvantage, instead of benefit, to the party accused. Some stations are so low, and so peculiarly characterised, that a jury of those, who were literally peers or of like condition with the prisoner, could not be assembled, nor would their character admit of their sitting in judgment on the life of a fellow-creature. The true meaning of a *trial by peers* is, that those who compose the jury are men, who, from their rank in life, have no privileges beyond what are enjoyed by the criminal whom they are to try; who are subject to the same laws with himself, and are therefore under no bias or temptation to

CHAP. I.

stretch them to his prejudice. The military law as contained in the Articles of War, regulates alike the conduct of the highest commissioned officer and the private soldier. The former is under no temptation to stretch or pervert that law to the prejudice of the latter, because its functions are alike explicit as to the duties of both, and the higher has no interest or advantage in abridging the privileges of the lower, but on the contrary, a natural incitement to maintain their common rights.

The votes of a majority are decisive.

It may be considered among the peculiar advantages of the mode of trial by Courts-Martial, that their decisions are the result, not of an unanimous concurrence of the opinions of all the members, but of a majority of them, in cases where the punishment does not affect the life of the criminal; and of two thirds of the members in capital cases.* Where unanimity is requisite, it is evident that in all cases of difficulty there must be a concession of the rights of private

* Article of War 87.

judgment, and an implicit acquiescence in the sentiments of some leading members of the jury; otherwise they never could agree upon a verdict. But this concession must often be attended with a violation of the dictates of conscience to individuals; and in cases where an individual either from scruple of conscience, or a worse motive, refuses to make that concession, an iniquitous verdict must be the consequence, if any verdict should be returned. In the sentences of Courts-Martial, no concession of right of private judgment is necessary. All the members of the court have their unbiassed judicative power; and even the influence of opinion is guarded against as far as possible, by the order in which the opinions and votes of the members are taken; the youngest member of the court being requested to give his opinion first, and the rest following in progressive seniority up to the president, who votes last.

The evidence must be reduced to writing.

It is likewise a material advantage of the trial by Courts-Martial, that the whole evidence is taken down in writ-

CHAP. I.

ing, in presence of the members of the court, who may at all times resort to the written proceedings, which at the close of the trial, and before sentence, are always read over to them, and compared with, and corrected by their own notes taken during the trial; so that every one of the members must be completely master of the whole body of the evidence.*

The court must adjourn from time to time

It may be deemed an important advantage of this mode of trial, that the court is compelled by law to adjourn its proceedings from day to day at an early hour, and may also at their own

* It has been the practice of the Author, while acting as Judge Advocate, to take down the proceedings and evidence in a rough way, on a book, or loose sheets of paper marked so as not to lose their connection; and during the adjournment of the court to copy them off in a fair hand, and read every morning at the opening of the court the whole proceedings of the day before, so that the members may correct them while every word and expression is fresh on the mind. This method besides insuring the greatest correctness enables the Judge-Advocate to lay the whole proceedings before the court at the moment they are ready to pronounce sentence, and when the sentence is fairly copied, the whole proceedings are ready for the signature of the President of the court.

CHAP. I.

discretion adjourn for any reasonable space of time, when farther deliberation is thought requisite; thus the attention of the members can never be harassed or worn out, or their judgment precipitated or rashly formed, it must therefore in all cases be the result of calm, attentive, and mature deliberation.

The Military Law does not interfere with the Civil.

The martial or military law, as contained in the Articles of War, does not in any respect either supercede or interfere with the civil and municipal laws of the country. On the contrary, it is expressly declared by the Articles of War, that "Whenever any commission-"ed officer or soldier shall be accused "of a capital crime, or of having used "violence, or committed any offence "against the persons or property of any "citizen of any of the United States, "such as is punishable by the known "laws of the land, shall upon applica-"tion duly made be delivered over to "the Civil Magistrate in order to bring "him or them to trial."* Hence it ap-

* Article of War 33.

CHAP. I.

pears, that soldiers are equally with all other classes of citizens bound to the same strict observance of the laws of the country, and the fulfilment of their social duties, and are alike amenable to the ordinary, civil, and criminal courts of the country, for all offences against those laws and breach of those duties.

The Military are required to give aid to the Civil.

The military law is in fact so much subordinate to the civil, that the military power is expressly required to give its aid for carrying the civil laws into effect and execution. The Articles of War* decree, that if any officer or soldier, &c. shall be accused of any capital crime, or any offence against the persons or property of any of the citizens of the United States, which is punishable by the known laws of the land, the commanding officer and officers of every regiment, troop, or company to which the person or persons so accused shall belong, are required to use their utmost endeavors to deliver over such accused person or per-

* Article of War 33.

CHAP. I.

sons to the civil magistrate, and likewise to be aiding and assisting the officers of justice in apprehending and securing the person or persons so accused, in order to bring him or them to trial. And this under a most severe penalty in case of refusal to give such aid, no less than being *ipso facto* cashiered.*

And is aided by it in its turn.

The civil power likewise gives its assistance to the military, in the apprehending of deserters; it being lawful for any constable or magistrate to apprehend or cause to be apprehended any person reasonably suspected to be a deserter, and to bring him before a Justice for examination; when if either by the party's confession, or by the testimony of one or more witnesses, or the Justice's own knowledge of the fact, the suspected person is found to be a deserter, the justice is authorised to commit him to jail, that he may be proceeded against according to law; and heavy penalties are enacted against

* Article of War 33.

CHAP. I.

all who conceal deserters, assist their escape, or receive, buy, or exchange their arms or clothes.*

So far, therefore, from there being any hostile interference between the civil and military powers of the State, we see it wisely provided, that the most perfect harmony shall subsist between them; and the provinces of each being distinctly defined, they are each required to lend an amicable aid to the other, in carrying their proper jurisdiction and authority into full effect.

The time limited for the prosecution of offences.

The military law, while it authorises every measure necessary for the punishment of offenders, is most strictly watchful to obviate every possible means of oppression, and to guard the administration of justice from every taint of malice, or of private resentment. The Articles of War, therefore, with equal wisdom and humanity provide, that "no "person shall be liable to be tried and "punished by a general court-martial

* See the Act of Congress, passed 16th April, 1802, fixing the Military Peace Estab. Sec. 19.

CHAP. I.

"for any offence which shall appear to "have been committed more than two "years before the issuing of the order "for such trial, unless the person by "reason of having absented himself or "some other manifest impediment, shall "not have been amenable to justice "within that period."* Indeed, justice requires, that all offences should become the subject of investigation and trial as speedily as possible after the time of their commission; nor is it consistent either with candor or equity to pass over in silence the first slight deviations from duty, arising perhaps from ignorance or inexperience, thus tempting the incautious offender to greater enormities, and afterwards to bring the former in aggrevation of his guilt; or even, as has been too frequently done, to make them parts of one accumulated charge against him. A procedure of this kind can receive no apology from the affected plea of humanely overlooking slight offences; for these offences,

* Article of War 88.

CHAP. I.

if so trivial as to merit no animadversion at the time, ought forever to be buried in oblivion, not treasured up for a future day of account; and if considerable enough to merit notice or censure, it is blamable in no mean degree to overlook them.

The President of the United States, or officer ordering the court, may order a revisal of the sentence.

As no sentence of a general court-martial is complete until it has received the approbation of the President of the United States, or the commander in chief to whom that power has been specially delegated, the president or such commander, disapproving of the sentence, may order the court to reconsider or review their proceedings, and recommend to them an alteration of their judgment; but as it is not consistent with the executive powers, under the constitution of the United States, actually to exercise any judicial authority, which belongs alone to the courts of justice; so the president can neither himself make any alteration in the sentence of such courts, nor commit that power to any other: all therefore, that it is competent for the President of the United

States to do, if the sentence of a court-martial shall not meet his approbation, is to order the court to review their proceedings.

The President's power of pardoning.

The President of the United States has the power of pardoning or remitting the sentences of courts-martial. This branch of the presidential prerogative is founded upon the *principle*, that as the president represents the body of the public, and possesses by delegation all its powers and rights with regard to the execution of the laws, all breaches against the public law are considered as offences against the people, and therefore to the president as their representative, it belongs of right to pardon offences against the public: and as it is not competent for any court by its own authority to dispense with the rigor of positive laws, however strongly the particular circumstances of a case may plead for such dispensation; so it is of the utmost consequence for the ends of justice, that an equitable power of this kind should be lodged with the chief magistrate, from whose hands it

CHAP. I.

is likely to be issued with the least hazard or suspicion of partial or impure motives.

Pardon is frequently extended to those who are condemned by a general court-martial, in consequence of a recommendation to mercy contained in the sentence of the court; who although they may have found themselves obliged by a sense of duty, or in consequence of the strict letter of the law, to pronounce a penal sentence, may yet be of opinion, that there are alleviating circumstances in the case which render the prisoner a proper object of clemency. In such case, the recommendation of the court is generally founded on the mention of those favorable circumstances. But in all cases whatever, the President of the United States has it in his power to grant either a conditional or free pardon, though there should be no recommendation from the court to that effect.

CHAP. II.

CHAPTER II.

Of Regimental and Garrison Courts-Martial.

Courts-Martial are either *general*, for the trial of the greater military crimes; or *regimental*, or *garrison*, for the cognizance of smaller offences.

Regimental Courts Martial.

The Articles of War provide, that "every officer commanding a regiment "or corps may appoint, for his own regiment or corps, courts-martial, to "consist of three commissioned officers, for the trial and punishment of "offences, not capital, and decide upon "their sentences. For the same purpose all officers commanding any of "the garrisons, forts, barracks, or other "places where the troops consist of different corps, may assemble courts-martial, to consist of three commissioned officers, and decide upon their "sentences."*

* Article of War 66.

CHAP. II.

Members.

The Articles of War contain no instruction or regulation with respect to the rank of these officers; but the usual practice is to appoint a captain and two subalterns, (if a captain can be conveniently spared) and in order that this duty may be equally shared, and all have the benefit of this necessary school of instruction; it is customary in every regiment for the adjutant to keep a regular roster for this as well as for all other regimental duties. The adjutant himself is frequently put upon this duty, and this practice has been condemned by some writers as irregular, upon the ground that the adjutant is to a regiment in many respects what a sheriff is to a county, and is appointed to superintend the execution of every judgment, and the inflicting of all punishments; and it is argued, that sheriffs are expressly prohibited from holding any pleas, or trying for any offences, so the same reason should hold against the appointment of adjutants to set on courts-martial; but this reasoning has but little solidity.

CHAP. II.

There is no ground in reason or in common sense, for presuming, that an adjutant should be a more partial or inequitous judge, because it his duty to see the sentence put in execution; and the adjutant is generally not the least qualified of the officers of a regiment to decide on matters of military duty and discipline.

Have no Judge-Advocates.

Regimental and garrison courts-martial being only competent to the trial of the lesser offences, or crimes which do not infer a capital punishment, and the cases that come before them not giving room for any intricacy of decision, or doubtful question of law, have not the aid of a judge-advocate to direct their proceedings.* The president, therefore, as well as the other members, have on that account much responsibility; they ought to be particularly careful that their proceedings be strictly con-

* It has latterly been a practice to appoint some young officer, to act as recorder, so as to instruct them in the mode of procedure in courts-martial, and at the same time render them familiar with their duty as members.

CHAP. II.

formable to military law and the practice of the army, as well as to the great principles of justice and equity. The members of regimental and garrison courts-martial take the same oaths as those of a general court-martial, and the evidence is in the same manner given upon oath.

Proceedings of regimental Courts-Martial.

The proceedings of regimental and garrison courts-martial must be accurately taken down in writing, either by the president or by a member of the court appointed by him, (this duty however is generally given to the youngest member) and the sentence must be regularly signed by the president.

Sentence.

No judgment of a regimental or garrison court-martial can be put in execution, until it shall have been confirmed by the commanding officer.* For the redressing all wrongs or injuries which an inferior officer or soldier may sustain from his superiors, the Articles of War declare, that "If any inferior officer, "or soldier, shall think himself wronged

Every inferior officer or soldier may have the benefit of a regimental court-martial.

* Article of War 65.

" by his captain or other officer, he " is to complain thereof to the com- " manding officer of the regiment, who " is *thereby* required to summon a re- " gimental court-martial, for the doing " justice to the complainant, from which " regimental court-martial, either party " may, if he thinks himself still aggriev- " ed, appeal to a general court-mar- " tial."* To check the frequency of ill-founded complaints, however, it is wisely enacted by the the same article, that " If upon a second hearing, the " appeal shall appear vexatious and " groundless, the person so appealing, " shall be punished at the discretion of " the said court-martial.

No commissioned officer amenable to regimental courts-martial.

It is material however to observe, that as no commissioned officer is properly amenable to the judgment or sentence of a regimental court-martial, the court on such complaint and enquiry, can only pronounce their opinion, whether the complaint is well or ill-founded; if they declare the latter, the complain-

* Article of War 35.

CHAP. II.

ant must either acquiesce in that opinion, or if he thinks himself still aggrieved, follow the mode of appeal to a general court-martial, as above prescribed. If the regimental court-martial declare the complaint to be well founded, the complainant may on that authority request a general court-martial, to take cognizance of the injury, and bring the offender to proper punishment.

CHAP. III. SECT. 1.

CHAPTER III.

Of the preliminaries to trial before Courts-Martial.

SECTION I.

OF PRINCIPALS AND ACCESSORIES.

THE actual commission of military crimes, such as mutiny, desertion, &c. and the advising, aiding, and abetting others in the commission of those crimes, are both punishable by the martial-law, and therefore all offenders either as principals or accessories in the commission of those crimes, are amenable to the jurisdiction of courts-martial. The distinction between principals in the commission of a crime, and accessories thereof, is distinctly pointed out by Sir William Blackstone.* "A "man may be a principal in an offence "in two degrees; a principal in the first "degree is he who is the actor or abso-

* Black. Com. b. 4. c. 3.

CHAP. III. SECT. 1.

" lute perpetrator of the crime; and in " the second degree, he who is present " aiding and abetting the fact to be done, " which presence need not be an actual " immediate standing by, within sight " or hearing of the fact; but there may " be also a constructive presence, as " when one commits a robbery or mur- " der and another keeps watch or guard " at some convenient distance. An " accessory is he who is not the chief " actor in the offence, nor present at its " performance, but is some-way con- " cerned therein, either before or after " the fact committed. An accessory " before the fact, is one, who being ab- " sent at the time of the crime commit- " ted, doth yet procure, counsel or com- " mand another to commit a crime. " The procuring of a felony to be com- " mitted, though by the intervention of " a third person, is being an accessory " before the fact. An accessory after " the fact may be, where a person know- " ing a felony to have been committed, " receives, relieves, comforts, or assists " the felony; and generally, any assist-

"ance whatever given to a felon to hinder his being apprehended, tried, or suffering punishment, makes the assister an accessory. To buy or receive stolen goods did not at common law constitute the being an accessory to the crime of theft, but was held a simple misdemeanor; but now, by statutes 5th Ann. c. 31, and 4th Geo. I. c. 11. all such receivers are made accessories."

Mutiny. Principals therein.

The crime of mutiny, the highest crime of which a soldier is capable, because it strikes immediately at the foundation of all military subordination, and by necessary consequence at the destruction of the State, is by martial-law punishable, when committed in its greatest extent, with death; and in its lesser modifications, with such other penalties, as a general court-martial may judge adequate to the degree of the offence.

Accessories to mutiny.

As the chief danger to this crime arises from its being shared or joined in by numbers, so it becomes a matter of high expediency, that the military law should guard most strictly against the

CHAP. III. SECT. 1.

communication of a contagion of so dangerous a nature. It is therefore wisely held to be the bounden duty of every soldier, to check this dreadful evil in its earliest stage, and not only to resist, and quell if possible, all its active appearances, but to give immediate information of every mutinous purpose that may come to his knowledge; and the breach of their duty by inactivity or silence, being justly held to be an approbation and acquiescence in the criminal designs, is declared to be punishable in the same degree with the actual crime. By the eighth Article of War, it is declared, that "Any officer, non-commissioned "officer, or soldier, who being present "at any mutiny or sedition, does not use "his utmost endeavours to suppress the "same, *or coming to a knowledge of any* "*intended mutiny*, does not without de-"lay give information thereof to his "commanding officer, shall be punish-"ed by the sentence of a court-martial "with *death* or otherwise, according to "the nature of his offence."

CHAP. III. SECT. 1.

Misbehaviour. Abandoning posts: accessories therein.

In like manner, the high military crime of misbehaviour in the face of an enemy, or the yet more atrocious, because more wilful and deliberate offence of betraying, abandoning, or delivering up any garrison, fortress, post, or guard, committed to the charge of an officer or soldier, is punished capitally or according to the measure of the crime, not only in the person, who actually commits it, but also in the accessory, as declared by the 52nd Article of War, that "Any officer or soldier, who shall "misbehave himself before the enemy, "run away, or shamefully abandon any "fort, post, or guard, which he or they "may be commanded to defend, *or speak* "*words inducing others to do the like*, "*&c.*" So likewise, the crime of desertion is punishable, not only in the person of the offender himself, but of the accessories. Article 23rd of the Rules and Articles of War, declare, that "any "officer or soldier who shall be con- "victed of having advised or persuad- "ed any other officer or soldier to de- "sert the service of the United States,

Accessories to desertion.

CHAP. III. SECT. 1.

"shall suffer death, or such other punishment as shall be inflicted upon "him by the sentence of a general "court-martial." And by Article 22nd, a soldier or non-commissioned officer enlisting himself in any other regiment, troop, or company, in which he last served, is held to be desertion, and is punishable as such; so the accessories to this offence are deemed equally guilty with the principals, it being declared, that "In case any officer shall knowingly receive and entertain such non-"commissioned officer or soldier, or "shall not after his being discovered to "be a deserter, immediately confine "him, and give notice thereof to the "corps in which he last served, the said "officer shall by a court-martial be ca-"shiered."

Harboring deserters, receiving clothes, arms, &c.

The harboring or concealing of deserters, purchasing of their arms, clothes, &c. is in the strictest sense an aiding or abetting of the crime; but it may be either a military or civil offence, according to the state or quality of the person who commits it. If committed by officers or soldiers, it is cognizable as a military crime by a court-martial, and is punished at the discretion of such tribunal. If committed by other persons, it falls under a special provision of the "Act fixing the Military Peace Establishment," which declares, that "every person who shall procure "or entice a soldier in the service of the "United States to desert, or who shall "purchase from any soldier his arms, "uniform, clothing, or any part thereof; "and every captain or commanding officer of any ship or vessel, who shall "enter on board such ship or vessel as "one of his crew, knowing him to have "deserted or otherwise, carry away any "such soldier, or shall refuse to deliver "him up to the orders of his commanding officer, shall upon legal conviction be fined at the discretion of any "court having cognizance of the same "in any sum not exceeding three hun- "dollars, or be imprisoned any term not "exceeding one year."*

* See Appendix.

CHAP. III. SECT. 1.

Sending challenges.

The crime of giving or sending a challenge, is punishable both in the principals and accessories; and of the latter, the military law distinguishes various sorts. The Articles of War ordain cashiering as the punishment of a commissioned officer who shall send or give a challenge, and corporal punishment for a non-commissioned officer or soldier guilty of the same offence.*

Accessories thereto.

If any commissioned officer or non-commissioned officer, commanding a guard, shall knowingly and willingly suffer any person whatsoever to go forth to fight a duel, he shall be punished as a challenger; and all seconds, promoters, and carriers of challenges, in order to duels, shall be deemed principals and be punished accordingly.†

Upbraiding for refusing a challenge.

As the practice of duelling is founded on mistaken sentiments of honor, and supported by false shame, it has been laudably endeavoured in the framing of laws and regulations for the army, to check the practice, by counteracting the

* Article of War 25. † Article of War 26.

CHAP. III SECT. 1.

principle. After announcing the punishments for giving or sending a challenge, it is therefore declared by the Articles of War, that "Any officer or "soldier, who shall upbraid another "for refusing a challenge, shall himself "be punished as a challenger," and a clause is added, solemnly acquitting all officers and soldiers of any disgrace or opinion of disadvantage, which might arise from their having refused to accept of challenges, as they will only have acted in obedience to the laws, and done their duty as good soldiers, who subject themselves to discipline.

Quelling frays.

All officers of what condition soever, have power to part and quell all quarrels, frays, and disorders, though the persons concerned should belong to another regiment, troop, or company; and either to order officers into arrest, or non-commissioned officers or soldiers into confinement, until their proper superior officers shall be acquainted therewith.* A great and extraordinary measure of

* Article of War, 27.

CHAP. III SECT. I.

authority is thus committed to every person who bears a commission as an officer, and which he ought to consider is to be his indispensible duty to exercise, whenever occasion shall require.

The army is held to be an individual body, of which all the parts must co-operate together in harmony; and for the perfect attainment of this end, the authority of officers is not limited to their own corps, or regiment, but is extended to every division or department of the army, whenever it is necessary to suppress this disorder. To enforce this ample authority, it is declared by the Articles of War, that "whosoever shall "refuse to obey such officer (though of "an inferior rank) or shall draw his "sword upon him, shall be punished at "the discretion of a general court-mar-"tial."*

Neglect of this duty.

Of a duty thus specially enjoined, and powerfully enforced, the neglect or breach of it must be esteemed a punishable offence. All officers and soldiers

* Article of War, 27.

witnessing quarrels, frays, and disorders, without using the authority and powers thus conferred upon them, must therefore be considered as aiding and abetting the principal offenders, and although no special penalty is prescribed for such offence by the Articles of War, they may be arraigned on that general article which ordains, that "all crimes "not capital, and all disorders and ne-"glects which officers and soldiers may "be guilty of to the prejudice of good "order and military discipline, though "not mentioned in the foregoing Arti-"cles of War, are to be taken cogni-"zance of by a general or regimental "court-martial, according to the nature "and degree of the offence, and be pu-"nished at their discretion."*

In general, therefore, it may be held as a military law, that all accessories to the commission of crimes or offences, either by the furnishing of actual aid or assistance to the principals by silently witnessing or concealing the crime, har-

* Article of War 99.

CHAP. III SECT. 1.

boring or assisting the escape of criminals, or barely neglecting that essential duty of every soldier, to promote to the utmost of his power the strict observance of good order and discipline, for which the martial law invests him with full authority, is guilty of a positive crime, and amenable for the punishment thereof to the cognizance and judgment of a court-martial.

The accessory and the principal may both be arraigned and tried at the same time, unless they shall demand a separate trial. It seems indeed to be consonant with justice, that the accessory should be a party in the trial with the principal, in order that he may have an opportunity of controverting the guilt of his supposed principal, and by consequence invalidating the charge against himself.

Notwithstanding it is an admitted principle in the cognizance of all crimes, that no man shall be brought twice into trial for the same offence, and there is an express *proviso* to that effect in the Articles of War, yet, although a man may be acquitted on his trial as an accessory, there is nothing to prevent his being afterwards arraigned and tried as a principal; as the offences are distinct, and the lesser cannot possibly involve the greater. But it is a matter of some doubt (says Sir William Blackstone) whether, if a man be acquitted as a principal, he can be afterwards indicted as accessory *before* the fact, since those offences are often very nearly allied, and therefore an acquittal of the guilt of one, may be an acquittal of the other also. But it is clearly held, that one acquitted as principal may be indicted as an accessory *after* the fact; since that is always an offence of a different species of guilt, principally tending to evade the public justice, and is subsequent in its commencement to the other.*

* Black. Com. b. 4th. c. 3.

CHAP. III. SECT. 2.

SECTION 2.

OF THE APPREHENDING OF CRIMINALS IN ORDER TO TRIAL.

Imprisonment in order to trial.

The Articles of War direct, that whenever any officer shall be charged with a crime he shall be arrested and confined in his barracks, quarters, or tent, and deprived of his sword by the commanding officer.* And they also declare that "non-commissioned officers and soldiers charged with crimes, "shall be confined until tried by a court-"martial, or released by proper autho-"rity."†

Nature & degree of arrests.

Although the martial law makes no mention of any difference in the nature of the arrest in order to trial, a difference is established by the custom of the army, according to the degree or measure of the crime: an officer accused of a capital crime, or any offence of which the penalty is so severe as to excite a natural temptation to escape from jus-

* Article of War 77. † Article of War 78.

tice ought to be detained in a state of confinement as secure as the closest civil imprisonment. If the offence be of a lighter nature, the presumption is, that the officer whose character is thus impeached must be solicitous to obtain a judicial investigation of his conduct, and he is therefore generally allowed to be in arrest at large, that is, to walk about within certain limits, without his sword, on his word of honor, to await the issue of a trial, or his enlargement by proper authority. The degree and measure of the arrest must however be entirely at the discretion of the commanding officer, who will in all cases regulate his conduct by the particular circumstances, and by the dictates of propriety and humanity.

Time of confinement.

The Articles of War decree, "that "no officer or soldier who shall be put "in arrest or imprisonment, shall con- "tinue in his confinement more than "eight days, or until such time as a "court-martial can be conveniently as- "sembled."* The latter part of this

* Article of War 79.

CHAP. III. SECT. 2.

clause evidently allows a latitude which is capable of being abused; but as in a free country there is no wrong without a remedy, the military law prescribes a mode of redress for all officers or soldiers, who conceive themselves injured by their commanding officer, which must always be sufficient for restraining of every act of injustice or oppression.

Penalty of refusing to keep prisoners, or releasing them without orders.

It is declared by the Articles of War that "no officer commanding a guard, "or provost martial, shall refuse to re-"ceive or keep any prisoner committed "to his charge by an officer belonging "to the forces of the United States; "provided the officer committing shall "at the same time deliver an account "in writing, signed by himself, of the "crime with which the said prisoner is "charged;"* and it also declares, "that "no officer commanding a guard, or "provost martial, shall presume to re-"lease any person committed to his "charge, without proper authority for

* Article of War 80.

" so doing, nor shall he suffer any per- " son to escape, on the penalty of being " punished for it by the sentence of a " court-martial."* " Every officer or " provost martial, to whose charge pri- " soners shall be committed, shall with- " in twenty-four hours after such com- " mitment, or as soon as he shall be " relieved from his guard, make report " in writing, to the commanding officer, " of their names, their crimes, and the " names of the officers who committed " them, on the penalty of being punish- " ed for disobedience or neglect, at the " discretion of a court-martial."†

Names of the prisoners to be returned.

Thus the liberty of the citizen under military law, in as far as is consistent with the ends of justice, seems to be guarded with precautions little inferior in their power and efficacy, to those which secure personal liberty under the civil laws of the state. The penalty of an officer's breaking his arrest, or leaving his confinement before he is set at liberty by the officer who confined him,

Breach of arrest.

* Article of War 81. † Article of War 82.

CHAP. III. SECT. 2.

or by a superior power, is declared to be cashiering by sentence of a general court-martial.*

* Article of War 77.

CHAPTER IV.

Of the Procedure and Form of Trial before a General Court-Martial.

SECTION 1.

OF THE ACCUSATION OR CHARGES.

The prosecution.

In all trials before a general court-martial, the Judge-Advocate sustains the prosecution in the name of *the United States of America;* and that either solely for the cognizance of a breach of the public military law, as for the trial of mutiny, desertion, &c. or in concurrence with a private prosecutor, who is *generally* a party that has individually suffered an injury by the aggressions and crime of the prisoner to be tried: we say *generally*, because it sometimes happens, that for the sake of public justice the individual who, from accidental situation, is best acquainted with the

CHAP. IV. SECT. 1.

particular circumstances of the crime to be tried, (though it be of a public nature) and who informs as to the matter of accusation, is requested to sustain in the court the character of prosecutor jointly with the Judge-Advocate, and to conduct the examination of the evidence on the part of the United States: a duty this of great moment, though not without its share of painful feelings to the individual who is called upon to discharge it: but feelings of private concern must ever give way to the greater ends of public justice; and the soldier or officer is unworthy of the character he bears, and indeed materially culpable, who does not consider that the allegiance he owes to his country and the maintainance of military law and discipline are his paramount obligations, to which he is bound to sacrifice every subordinate and selfish consideration. A prosecution may be brought in a court-martial at the suit of a person who is himself not subject to military jurisdiction, provided the offence be of a military nature, and committed by a person under the military law.*

The charges.

In whatever terms the accusation in the charges may be conceived, it is necessary,

1st. That the crime or offence be clearly specified and expressed; and the act or acts of guilt pointedly charged against the prisoner.

2nd. That the time and place when and where the crime was committed, be set forth with all possible certainty and precision.

As all crimes admit of certain degrees and modifications of guilt, it is essentially necessary to the ends of justice, that any prisoner who is to undergo trial for a crime, should be apprised of the extent and degree of guilt with which he stands charged, and of the particular facts of which the prosecutor

* The surgeon of a British regiment was lately (Dec. 1799) prosecuted before a general court-martial, at Norwich, *at the suit of a coroner*, for neglect of duty in not paying proper attention, to a sick soldier of that regiment, who died of a dysentary in the hospital. The defendant was honorably acquitted, and the sentence approved by the king.

CHAP. IV. SECT. 1.

means to bring evidence against him, in order that he may have a fair opportunity of invalidating the proof of those facts by contrary evidence. As therefore, in a civil court of justice, it would not be sufficient to state in the indictment that the party is guilty of murder, without specifying the particular act of killing or slaying a certain person, and the manner in which the slaughter was committed, so in trials by courts-martial the charge must contain a distinct specification of the criminal act or acts. Thus if the crime be mutiny, it is not sufficient that the charges bear that A.B. is guilty of mutiny. The particular acts of mutinous conduct in the prisoner must be clearly and distinctly enumerated; as entering forcibly and with arms into a guard-house and releasing a prisoner; using certain specified traitorous expressions against the President of the United States, or Vice-President thereof; or contemptuous and disrespectful language towards a superior officer, or offering such and such acts of violence against him; urging his fellow-soldiers to resist military orders; persuading them to revolt to the enemy, &c. In like manner, if the crime is abandoning or betraying a garrison, fortress or post, not only must the particular fortress, post, or garrison be distinctly specified, but the special act of treachery described, and the manner in which it was committed.

There is one class of offences in which a distinct specification of the criminal act or acts is more particularly necessary. It is ordained by the Rules and Articles of War, that "Any commissioned officer convicted before a general court-martial, of conduct unbecoming an officer and a gentleman, *shall be dismissed* the service."* As this is a crime of great latitude of interpretation, and admitting both of an infinite variety of the acts from which such misbehaviour may be inferred, and possibly often of a difference of opinion with regard to the degree of guilt that may be attached to such acts; it is evident

* Article of War, 83.

CHAP. IV. SECT. I.

that much injustice would be done to any prisoner who should be arraigned before a court-martial, upon a general charge of "conduct unbecoming an officer and a gentleman," without any specification of the facts which were deemed to constitute such gross misbehaviour, and which possibly the prisoner if apprised of them, might either totally disapprove, or shew that they admitted of such extenuation from circumstances as might alleviate, or altogether exculpate from the charge. As the Articles of War do not particularly enjoin that the charge shall contain a clear or distinct specification of the facts, it might perhaps be argued that such specification is not essentially necessary; and it must be owned that in practice it has too frequently been dispensed with, and a general charge allowed as of mutiny, disobedience of orders, disrespectful conduct to superior officers, &c. But the generality of such charges altho' if not absolutely reprobated by the military law, or amount to a voidance or annulling of the indictment, affords in every case a competent and weighty objection upon the part of the prisoner, which he may urge to the effect of having the charge rendered specially by a pointed detail from the prosecutor of the particular facts on which it is founded: and this requisition by the prisoner which is founded in justice, no court-martial can legally refuse. In any case, therefore, it is most advisable to prevent all objection by a clear specification of the facts, in the charges furnished to the prisoner, on which he is to be arraigned. The charges must clearly designate and mark out the person of the prisoner by his name, surname, rank or station, and regiment or corps to which he belongs, &c. as A.B. captain, lieutenant, ensign, sergeant, corporal, or private, &c. in the regiment of, &c.

Specification of the time and place.

The same minuteness and precision ought to be observed in specifying the *time* and *place* when and where the facts charged were committed, when it is possible to be thus particular; for such specification may in most cases be es-

CHAP. IV. SECT. 1.

sentially necessary towards the prisoner's defence.

One of the most complete and conclusive proofs of exculpation is an *alibi*, that is, when convincing evidence is produced to the court, that the prisoner was in a different place, at the time when the crime is charged to have been committed. As to the circumstance of *place*, it is in all cases possible for the prosecutor to be most pointed and specific, and therefore such specification can never be dispensed with in the framing of the charge. But with regard to time there cannot always be the same certainty and precision. Witnesses with no intention to violate the truth, may from the defect of memory, vary in their testimony as to hours, days, time of the day, name of the month, &c. and yet be most pointed and accurate as to the acts committed. The prosecutor therefore wanting the same absolute certainty for his information, is allowed some latitude with respect to time; and provided the charge is in other respects sufficiently precise, he may charge the fact or facts to have been committed on such a day of such a month, or on one or other of the days of that month or of the month immediately following. But as this is an indulgence granted only from necessity, so in no case when it is possible for the prosecutor to mark the time with certainty and precision ought he to be allowed such latitude as that above-mentioned, as it deprives the prisoner of all opportunity of proving an *alibi*. Although no crimes or offences are cognizable by a court-martial, unless what are either specially declared to be such by the Articles of War, or fall under the general description of disorder and neglects, to the prejudice of military discipline; it is not customary nor is it necessary, in drawing up the charges against an offender to refer to any particular Article of War of which he has been guilty of a breach. Such references can answer no good purpose, but might often lead to cavelling, and captious objections. The specification of the criminal act is sufficient intimation

It is not necessary to refer specially to the Articles of War.

CHAP. III. SECT. 1.

to the prisoner that his offence is considered by the prosecutor to be a breach of the military law, and it is always competent for him to dispute its relevancy, and to call upon the prosecutor and shew in what respect it falls under the prohibition of the law.

A copy of the charges must be furnished the prisoner.

A true copy of the charges on which the prisoner is to be tried must be furnished to him by the Judge-Advocate in such time before the meeting of the court that he may have full opportunity of preparing himself for his defence, that is, collecting such evidence, either oral or written, as may be necessary for his exculpation, or in rebutting the proofs of the charge, and for the advising with his counsel, on all points touching the conduct of the trial, objections to the members, competency of the witnesses, &c.

After the charges have been thus far furnished to the prisoner, it is not competent for the Judge-Advocate or the prosecutor, to make any alteration on them either in substance or in form, when they come before the court. If a

CHAP. IV. SECT. 2.

material alteration occurs to be made before trial, the consent of the commander in chief, or of the person on whose order the trial is to proceed, must be obtained for that alteration of which likewise the prisoner is entitled to have the most timely notice that can be given to him.

SECTION 2.

FORM OF CONSTITUTING THE COURT.

Authority under which the court is held.

GENERAL courts-martial are convened either by the direct authority of the President of the United States, or by order of the commander in chief, or other officer having the power to assemble general courts-martial.

All trials before courts-martial, like those in the civil courts of judicature, are conducted publicly, and with open doors; and in order that this publicity of trial may in no case be attended with

CHAP. IV. SECT. 2.

tumult or indecorum of any kind, the court is authorised by the Rules and Articles of War* to punish, at their discretion, all riotous and disorderly proceedings, or menacing words, signs, or gestures, used in their presence.

The prisoner brought into court.

The president and the whole of the members of the court, being assembled, on the day appointed for its meeting, and intimation having been previously given for all the necessary witnesses to attend, the prisoner is brought into court, and called to the bar by his name; and although until that period, he may have been in close confinement, even in irons, he must appear then unfettered, and without bonds of any kind; unless (as the antient law and customs authorise) when there is danger of escape, or rescue.†

The Judge-Advocate now reads in an *audable* voice, the warrant or order, for holding the court. He then calls over the names of the members of the court, who are desired to take their places, ac-

* Article of War 76.

† Hawkin's Pleas Crown

cording to their rank in the army, and the dates of their commissions, arranging themselves in that order, alternately on the right and left hand of the president.—*Vide Plate.*

Privilege of challenging members.

The Judge-Advocate then demands of the prisoner, whether he has any objection against, or challange to make of any of the members present, and if he have, he is required to state his cause of challenge, on which, the president must order the court to be cleared, and the members will then deliberate on the import and validity of the same. In the trial of crimes before a civil court, the law allows to the prisoner a right of *peremptory* challenge; that is, of positively disclaiming such and such persons (to a certain number) to be of the special jury, without any cause or objection shewn.

Grounds of challenges.

In courts-martial, however, there is no such liberty allowed. The prisoner must assign his cause of challenge, of the relevancy or validity of which, the members are themselves the judges, and no challenge to more than one member

CHAP. IV. SECT. 2.

at a time can be received by the court.*

The most valid causes of challenge, are suspicion of prejudice, or malice, and *infamous character*. The suspicion of prejudice may reasonably be inferred against a member, from the circumstances of near relation to any person or party injured by the crime of the prisoner, or having any interest in the cause, whereby he may be led to wish the condemnation of the prisoner. As such causes of prejudice are various in their degree, it is in the breast of the members, as judges of their validity, to give them what weight they may conceive they are entitled to; nor can any general rule of decision be prescribed.

As previous to the assembling of a general court-martial, it sometimes happens, that a court of enquiry is appointed, for the purpose of determining whether there appear sufficient grounds for bringing the person accused, to trial; and it is allowed to such courts of en-

* Article of War, 71.

CHAP. IV. SECT. 2.

quiry, to call before them, and examine, all witnesses, both in support of, and defence against the accusation, and report their opinion of the grounds of charge; it has been questioned, whether the members of such court of enquiry are thereby incapacitated from being afterwards appointed to sit on a court-martial, for the trial of a prisoner, on whose cause they have already reported their opinion. A court of enquiry bearing a near affinity to a grand jury, and the law being precise on that point, that no grand juror who has found a bill of indictment against a prisoner, can be a member of the petty jury, on the trial of that prisoner, or even the trial of another, wherein the same matter is in question. It seems to be thence, with much reason, concluded, that it is sufficient ground for challenging the member of a general court-martial, who had given his opinion of the cause in a previous court of enquiry. For although the members of a court of enquiry do not actually pronounce a sentence upon the cause, but only re-

CHAP. IV. SECT. 2.

port their opinion, whether there appear sufficient ground for bringing the accused person to trial; yet even that opinion is derogatory from absolute impartiality, a natural bias thence arising to support and justify it on the final trial.

So jealous is the law of the perfect impartiality of jurors, that it is allowed to be a good cause of challenge, that the juror has been heard to give his opinion before-hand, that the party is guilty,* and a similar ground of challenge against the member of a court-martial would without doubt be sustained. Much more would it be a sufficient ground of challenge against the member of a general court-martial, in an appeal from the sentence of a regimental court, that the same person had been one of the judges in the latter.

The causes of challenge impossible to be overruled, are the charge of corruption or bribery, verified by competent proof; and malice or hostile enmity

* 2 Hawkins, 418.

expressed by word, or deed against the prisoner. Infamous character is likewise a most relevant ground of challenge; but as this objection admits of no precise definition or description, it would be necessary wherever it is moved, that the fact or reasons on which it is founded should not only be specified, but proved. Thus a member may be reasonably challenged on the head of infamous character, who has been tried and convicted of a crime; but the proof of that fact must be produced in court, that is, the record of his conviction.

The privilege of challenge is mutual to the prisoner and to the prosecutor; for there may be sources of prejudice in favor of the prisoner as well as against him, and urgent motives that may sway to acquit, as well as to condemn.

Members sworn.

Where the prisoner and prosecutor decline to challenge any of the members, where the causes of challenge have been disallowed, the Judge-Advocate proceeds to administer to the members of the court, the oath prescribed

CHAP. IV. SECT. 2.

by the Articles of War. The oath is taken by each person holding up his right hand, and repeating the words after the Judge-Advocate. After the oath has been administered to all the members, the President administers to the Judge-Advocate the particular oath of secrecy to be taken by him.

The oath to be taken by the president and members contains a twofold obligation of secrecy.—1st. That they will not divulge the sentence of the court, until it shall be published by proper authority, and 2nd. That they shall not disclose or discover the vote or opinion of any particular member of the court-martial, unless required to give evidence thereof by a court of justice in a due course of law.*

Both these obligations have their foundation in reason and good policy. No sentence of a general court-martial is complete or final, until it has been duly approved. Until that period, it is strictly speaking, no more than an opi-

* Article of War, 69.

nion, which is subject to alteration or revisal. In this interval the communication of that opinion could answer no ends of justice, but might, in many cases tend to frustrate and defeat them. The obligation to perpetual secrecy, with respect to the votes or opinions of the particular members of the court, is likewise founded on the wisest policy. The members of a court-martial cannot boast of the same independence of the executive, and consequent immunity from influence, as the judges in the ordinary courts of law. The officers who compose a military tribunal, are necessarily dependant for their preferment on the president and his ministers: They are even in some degree under the influence of their commander in chief: Powerful motives of opinion! which might sometimes lead a weaker mind astray from the direct path of justice. This danger is therefore best obviated by the confidence and security which every man possesses, that his particular opinion is never to be divulged. Another reason of yet stronger nature, is,

CHAP. IV. SECT. 2.

that the individual members of the court may not be exposed to the resentment of parties and their connections, which can hardly fail to be excited by those sentences which it is often necessary for courts-martial to pronounce. It may be necessary for officers, in the course of their duty, daily, to associate, and frequently be sent on the same command or service, with a person against whom they have given an unfavorable vote, or opinion, in a court-martial. The publicity of these votes or opinions would create the most dangerous animosities, equally fatal to the peace and security of individuals, and prejudicial to the public service.

The oath of the Judge-Advocate.

The oath which is taken by the Judge-Advocate, contains the same obligation to secrecy, except so far as it relates to the person who has the approving of the sentence of the court, to whom it may be of material importance previously to that approbation, that the opinion of the Judge-Advocate, with regard to the propriety, justice and legality of the sentence of the court should be known.

The Judge-Advocate is, however, bound by oath, as well as the members of the court, to maintain the strictest secrecy with regard to the votes or opinions of individuals, for the same reasons of expediency and good policy.

The oaths are to be adminis-tered but once only.

The oaths which are taken previously to the proceeding of the court-martial to any trial, form in fact the essentials by which the court is constituted: they therefore create an obligation, which is binding on all the members, until it is finally dissolved. It is on that account unnecessary and improper (for all unnecessary oaths are improper) for the same court-martial to repeat the ceremony of taking these oaths for every new trial. The writers who have maintained this opinion, have grounded it on the words of the charge given by the Judge-Advocate, previous to the oath of the members, "you shall well and truly try and determine, according to evidence, the matter now before you." But in the first place, the term

CHAP. IV. SECT. 2.

matter being general, will apply to every subject of criminal prosecution, which is to be tried by the court, and in the second place, the words of the oath taken by the members is entirely general, applying to their duty as judges, with which character they continue invested until all the trials are finished, and the court dissolved. It has been urged in opposition to this doctrine, that the privilege of challenging the members of the court, being competent to every prisoner, and custom requiring that such challenge should be made before the members are sworn; if that form were not to be repeated in the commencement of every new trial, none could avail themselves of the right of challenge, but the first who was arraigned. But there is no reason of justice or common sense, that should preclude a person from challenging, on sufficient cause, any of the members *after* the court is sworn, provided he had no opportunity of moving his objection *before* the form was gone through. An objection cannot be said to be waved, which the objector had no power of urging: Nay, let the case be supposed, that a prisoner had positively declined to challenge any of the members of the court, as being ignorant at the time of any competent or just objection, in consequence of which, all the members are solemnly sworn, and the trial is entered upon, and afterwards a most just cause of challenge comes to the prisoner's knowledge, emerging perhaps from the evidence itself, can any doubt be entertained, that such challenge would not avail the prisoner? It may, in practice, be held incompetent to challenge a jury-man, after he is sworn; but admitting this to be the practice, with respect to juries, (for which however, there appears no sufficient reason) the analogy does not hold good between a jury, which is chosen anew for every particular trial, and whose functions begin and end with that trial, and a court-martial, which, when many offences are to be tried, is to hear, examine, and to give

CHAP. IV. SECT. 3.

judgment in all matters which shall be brought before them.

SECTION 3.

ARRAIGNMENT AND TRIAL OF THE PRISONER.

Incident to arraignment.

THE court being now regularly constituted, and every preliminary form gone through, the Judge-Advocate, as prosecutor for the United States, desires the prisoner to listen to the charge or charges exhibited against him, which he reads with an audible voice; and then the prisoner is asked, "whether he is guilty or not guilty of the matter of accusation."

Thus arraigned, the prisoner may either 1. *stand mute*, that is, refuse to answer, or answer foreign to the purpose; 2. *confess* the fact of which he is accused, or 3. plead *not guilty* to the charge.

CHAP. IV. SECT. 3.

Standing mute.

It was formerly the practice of our courts-martial, in case the prisoner stood mute from obstinacy, and deliberate design, or answered foreign to the purpose, to proceed against him as if he had regularly pleaded guilty; particularly after endeavouring with wisdom and temperance to overcome his obstinacy, by setting forth the dreadful consequence which awaited him. But it is now humanely ordained in the Articles of War, "when any prisoner arraigned "before a general court-martial, shall, "from obstinacy and deliberate design, "stand mute, or answer foreign to the "purpose, the court may proceed to "trial and judgment as if the prisoner "had regularly pleaded not guilty.*"

When an interpreter is necessary.

A prisoner's ignorance of the language in which he is arraigned, and in which the trial is to be conducted, may bring him into a predicament somewhat similar to that of standing mute to the charge. In such case it is necessary that a neutral person of ability and dis-

* Article of War, 70.

CHAP. IV. SECT. 3.

cretion, who is equally skilled in both languages, should be sworn, to interpret between the prisoner and the prosecutor and court. This interpreter must, in in the first place, explain to him, distinctly the import and substance of the charge, and deliver to the court his answer to the accusation; and during the whole course of the trial, he must translate, for the benefit of the prisoner, the import of the evidence of each of the witnesses, and put such questions as the prisoner shall suggest, either in the way of cross-examination of the evidence for the prosecution, or directly as exculpatory proof.

Confessing the crime.

2. If the prisoner plainly and explicitly confess the crime with which he is charged, nothing remains for the court, but to pronounce judgment; but as in such circumstances, the awarding of a capital or most rigorous sentence is peculiarly painful, the court, not only for the ease of their own minds, but in humanity to the prisoner, who may, perhaps, be influenced by an illusive hope of mercy, will not willingly record

such confession, or preclude the unhappy criminal from ample time and opportunity of retracting it: Indeed, if a criminal court is influcnced, as it ever ought to be, by the equitable consideration of duly proportioning punishment to the degrees of offence, reason and humanity will plead with equal force in their breasts for a mitigation of the doom of a penitent, and confessing offender. The essence of a crime is the intention with which it is committed, and the malignancy of that intention is the measure of its atrocity. But most assuredly the mind of that offender is less obstinately and inveterately malignant, who under a strong impression and conciousness of his guilt, explicitly avows it, and throws himself upon the mercy of his judges, than of him, who, guilty of the same crime, has the hardihood to persist in a denial of his guilt, and boldly to abide the issue of a trial.

General issue, or not guilty.

3. But the most customary plea of a prisoner, and always the most desirable, is the general issue, or that of *not guilty* of the charge; and this plea

CHAP. IV. SECT. 3.

must be simple, and without qualification or justification, that is, an absolute denial on the part of the prisoner of the crime which is laid to his charge; this cannot be better explained than in the words of Sir William Blackstone, which, though relating strictly speaking to trial before civil courts of justice, are however applicable to courts-martial. "In case of an indictment for "felony or treason, there can be no "special justification put in by way of "plea: As on an indictment for murder, "a man cannot plead that it was in his "own defence, against a robber on the "highway, or a burgler, but he must "plead the general issue, not guilty, "and give this special matter in evi-"dence, and the jury upon that evidence "will take notice of any defensive mat-"ter, and give their verdict accordingly, "as effectually as if it were or could be "specially pleaded. So that this is, "upon all accounts, the most advanta-"geous plea for the prisoner.*"

* Black. b. 4, c. 26.

CHAP. IV. SECT. 3.

Pleas in bar of trial.

But a prisoner who neither stands mute, confesses the crime, nor pleads not guilty to the charge, may immediately upon his arraignment, offer certain pleas in bar of the trial, as that he has been formerly tried for the same individual act, or acts of crime, which, if verified by production of the record of his acquittal or conviction, or even by other sufficient evidence, must effectually quash the trial. It may easily be understood, however, that the plea of a former acquittal can be of no avail, if the new trial is brought in appeal of the judgment of the court which had pronounced the sentence of acquittal. A pardon of the crime for which the prisoner is arraigned, is likewise a valid plea in bar of the trial: Nor, is it to be doubted that a promise or assurance of mercy, given on condition of becoming evidence against an accomplice, or a criminal who is tried for the same offence, would be admitted by the court as an effectual bar of the trial of the person who pleads it and verifies his plea.

CHAP. IV. SECT. 3.

But with respect to these pleas in bar of trial, it is proper to remark, that although, if admitted, they are conclusive in favor of the prisoner, they are not, if repelled, conclusive against him who urges them; that is to say, if the court shall determine against him on the plea in bar, he shall not thereupon be immediately convicted, but shall still be at liberty to resort to the general issue, or the plea of not guilty of the charge. For the law, says Blackstone, "allows "many pleas by which a prisoner may "escape death, but only one plea in consequence of which it can be inflicted, "viz. on the general issue, after an impartial examination and discussion of "the facts.*"

Objections to jurisdiction.

A prisoner, moreover, may validly object to the jurisdiction of the court, if it appear that they have no proper authority for taking cognizance of the crime; as, if a soldier were arraigned before a court-martial for a crime cognizable only by the civil courts, or brought

* Black. b. 4, c. 26.

before a regimental court-martial, for a capital offence. It would be likewise a good objection, that the court did not consist of the requisite number of members, or that these were not of the requisite rank to sit upon the trial of the prisoner; as, if a lieutenant or ensign were appointed to sit on the trial of a field officer, particularly when an officer of a higher degree could have been appointed a member.*

Trial.

The prisoner having pleaded the general issue of not guilty, the prosecutor proceeds to produce his evidence in support of the charges, by the examination of witnesses, and the production of such written documents as tend to substantiate and prove the matters of accusation; a list of the witnesses having been furnished to the prisoner, previously to the trial, that he may be aware of, and have full time to deliberate on any objection that may be against their admissibility, or prepare himself to en-

* Article of War, 75.

CHAP. IV. SECT. 3.

counter their testimony by contrary evidence.

If the accusation resolves itself into a variety of distinct articles or charges, the court will allow the prisoner his option, whether to urge his defence and examine evidence seperately to each article, or to enter upon the general proof of exculpation after the prosecutor has gone through the whole of his evidence in support of the charges. The former mode of procedure seems the more eligible when the prisoner is charged with several distinct and seperate crimes; as if, for example, the same person were charged with disobedience of orders, embezzling of public stores, and encouraging mutiny. The latter mode seems preferable, when the charges, though consisting of seperate acts, either amount to the same crime or are intimately connected, as false muster or returns, made at different times, various acts of embezzling of pay, of clothing, &c. &c.

Examination of witnesses.

In order to maintain regularity in the proceedings of the court, the witnesses in support of the charges are first examined by the Judge-Advocate, or prosecutor, and when he has finished his interrogatories the prisoner is allowed to cross-question, that is, to put any relevant questions that may occur to him, arising from and relative to the evidence already given. When the prisoner has finished his cross-questioning, the court may put any questions they may think proper, in explanation of what has already been sworn, or in farther proof of the articles of charge.

It is of importance that this rule, which is common to all criminal courts, should be strictly observed. A deviation from it deranges the chain of evidence, and introduces perplexities and confusion in the record of the proceedings.

Each witness previous to his examination, is sworn by the Judge-Advocate, to declare the truth, the whole truth, and nothing but the truth,

The evidence must be taken down in writing.

The Judge-Advocate who is recorder of the court, takes down the whole of the evidence in writing from the

CHAP. IV. SECT. 3.

mouth of the witness; beginning each testimony with the name and designation of the witness, and noting whether he be a witness for the prosecutor or for the prisoner, as "A.B. captain "in the .... regiment of infantry, a "witness for the prosecution, solemnly "sworn and examined, says as follows:" The evidence is most usually taken down in questions and answers, each interrogatory denoting the party who puts it; as, Ques. by the Prosecutor; Ques. by the Court; Ques. by the Prisoner. Sometimes, however, the witness gives his testimony in way of narrative; in which manner it must likewise be taken down in writing, the recorder adhering as nearly as possible to the very words of the witness.

No witness is permitted to read his evidence to the court; for this might give room for subornation of evidence, against which every court is most anxious to guard, by the preliminary questions, whether the witness has been instructed what to say, or received any reward for giving his testimony. Although however, the witness is not allowed to read his evidence, it is not illegal or improper, in circumstantial cases, or in cases where the dates are to be detailed, or matters of account, for the witness to make use of written notes, for the aid of his memory, and for the greater precision of his testimony.

Witnesses must be examined apart.

The more effectually to guard the purity of the evidence, those who are cited to appear as witnesses are not allowed to be present in the court during the examination of any of the previous witnesses, as this circumstance would of itself afford a valid objection to their testimony, being a species of subordination. It is proper, therefore, that in the commencement of the trial, and indeed in the outset of every day's proceedings, the Judge-Advocate should give warning to all who are cited as witnesses, and who may chance to be present, to retire and not to enter the court till they are officially called upon to be sworn.

Counsel if admitted in a court-martial.

Courts-martial being in general composed of men of ability and discretion,

CHAP. IV. SECT. 3.

but who, from the nature of their profession and general mode of life, are not to be supposed versed in legal subtilties or abstract and sophistical distinctions; and the cases that come before them giving rise to few questions of law; it has been considered as founded in established usage, that counsel or professional lawyers are not allowed to interfere in their proceedings, or by argument or pleading of any kind to endeavor to influence either their interlocutory opinions or final judgment. This is a most wise and important regulation, nor can any thing tend more to secure the equity and wisdom of their decisions: for lawyers being in general as utterly ignorant of military law and practice, as the members of courts-martial are of civil jurisprudence and of the forms of the ordinary courts; so nothing could result from the collision of such warring and contradictory judgment, but inextricable embarrasment, or rash, ill-founded and illegal decisions.

Although it is thus wisely provided, that professional lawyers shall not

CHAP. IV. SECT. 3.

interfere in the proceedings of courts-martial, by pleading or argument of any kind, it is at the same time not unusual for a prisoner to request the court to allow him the aid of counsel to assist him in his defence, either in the proper conduct of exculpatory proof, by suggesting witnesses, or in drawing up in writing a connected statement of his defence, and observations on the general import of the evidence. This benefit the court will never refuse to a prisoner; because under those unhappy circumstances, the party may either want ability to do justice to his own cause, or may be deserted by that presence of mind which is necessary to command and bring into use such abilities as he may actually possess. In this situation, however, the prisoner's consel, who properly understands his duty, will see it is his part not to embarras, to tease or perplex the court, but rather to conciliate their favor, by wisely regulating the conduct of his client; nor to force the axioms and rules of the civil courts upon a military tribunal, but to instruct himself in that law which regulates their procedure, and accommodate himself to their forms and practice.

When the evidence in support of the charges is closed, the prisoner sometimes judges it proper to submit to the court, either verbally, or in writing, a general statement of those defences which he means to support by evidence. He then enters upon his exculpatory proof, by examining such witnesses as he thinks material to refute the preceding evidence, or to establish his general character and good behaviour, or by producing written documents to these effects. The examination of the exculpatory witnesses, is conducted in a similar manner to that of the evidence of the prosecution. The prisoner first interrogates his own witnesses, putting his question, either himself, or by the mouth of the Judge-Advocate. When his interrogations are ended, the prosecutor is entitled to cross-question the evidence; and finally, the court put all questions to the witnesses that appear to them proper for bringing out the truth.

When the whole evidence on both sides is closed, the prisoner may, if he thinks proper, demand leave of the court, to sum up, either verbally, or in a written statement, the general matter of his defence, and to bring into one view the import of the proof of the charges, with such observations as he conceives are fitted to weaken its force; and the result of the evidence in defence, aided by any arguments that is capable of giving it weight. To this statement on the part of the prisoner, the prosecutor has a right to make a reply; and under this privilege, he may either recapitulate, methodise the import of his evidence, and strengthen it by pertinent argument, or shew the weakness and insufficiency of the proof in exculpation; and here in strict regularity the trial ends. But if the prisoner shall, in his defence, have impeached the credibility of any of the witnesses for the prosecution, it is competent for the prosecutor to re-establish their character

CHAP. IV. SECT. 3.

by new evidence, or if the prisoner in his defence, shall have introduced any new matter encountering the evidence of the charge, but to which that evidence was not directed, the prosecutor is allowed to examine the witnesses relating to this new matter; as for instance, a prisoner is charged with an act of mutiny, and the charge is clearly proved, but the prisoner in his defence alleges, and adduces evidence to shew that he was compelled by others to the commission of the act, against his own will, and at the hazard of his life. This being new matter to which the former evidence for the prosecution does not in the least apply, the prosecutor is allowed to rebut it, by the examination of witnesses, or the production of such documents as he thinks fit to disprove it. In such cases, it is customary for the court to allow the prisoner the liberty of a rejoinder, or answer to the prosecutor's reply; an indulgence to which, in ordinary cases, he is not entitled.

CHAPTER V.

Of Evidence.

In the trial of military crimes by courts-martial, the rules of evidence, which have their foundation in the principles of justice and of reason, are the same that apply to the trial of crimes before the civil courts. It is therefore, of essential consequence, that the general doctrine of the law of evidence should be understood by all military persons, who may either be called on to discharge the important functions of judges, in a military tribunal, or to sustain the more painful character of parties in its proceedings.

Definition of evidence.

Evidence is that which either proves and demonstrates, or which renders highly probable and worthy of credit to a court or jury, the facts or points in issue before them.

CHAP. V.

What has no tendency to establish the facts or points in issue, is therefore no evidence, and ought not to be admitted by a court.

But in circumstantial and presumptive evidence, circumstances which have an immediate and direct tendency to prove the very facts in issue, may have an indirect and consequential tendency to that effect, and therefore not to be disallowed by a court, provided the party who urges them shall make their consequences apparent.

Evidence is of two kinds: viz. 1. *viva voce*, or parole-evidence, given by witnesses in court; and 2. written evidence, by records, deeds, and other authentic and probative papers. Of these two species of proof, it is necessary to treat separately, first premising certain rules relative to evidence in general.

General rules relative to evidence.

It is a general rule, that in all cases, the best evidence of which the matter is capable, shall be resorted to, provided that evidence can be brought. If that be impossible, the court will

CHAP. V.

require the best evidence that can be had. "For if it be plainly seen in the "nature of the transaction, that there "is some more evidence that doth not "appear, the very not producing it is "a presumption that it would have de- "tected something more than appears "already; and though the mind does "not acquiesce in any thing lower than "the utmost evidence the fact is capa- "ble of.*"

All evidence for and against the facts in issue, are to be weighed, and judgment given according to that which predominates. In the balancing of contrary evidence, the mind is to be guided by no other rule than this, of whatever nature it be, which produces the strongest belief. Thus, if one single witness of sufficient credibility, who had the best opportunity of knowing the truth, shall swear positively to the fact, and his testimony shall be encountered by two other witnesses, whose credibility is more suspicious, or whose

* Baron Gilbert's Laws of Evidence.

CHAP. V.

opportunity of knowledge was not so great; the testimony of the witness producing stronger proof than that of the others, ought to predominate.

On the same principle, a testimony which is precise and circumstantial, must outweigh that which is less particular or minute, and goes only to a general fact; because the former implies more attentive observation, and more pointed recollection, and therefore creates a stronger belief.

From this principle, likewise, it follows, that positive evidence must outweigh that which is negative; for the former being the result of attention and observation of the facts, can never be encountered, or disproved by that which may have arisen merely from the want of such attention and observation. Thus, supposing two credible witnesses shall depose pointedly to certain words spoken by A. as, that he called B. a scoundrel; and two or three other witnesses of equal credibility shall swear, that though high words were used, they did not hear that particular expression; the former evidence ought to predominate over the latter.

The weight of a witness' evidence does not depend altogether upon the words which he utters upon oath, but often greatly upon the manner in which his testimony has been delivered. Thus the testimony of a witness who appears evidently to be influenced by his passions, in giving his evidence on either side of a cause, is of much less weight when swearing to facts which favor that side, than the evidence of another who exhibits no such bias; and consequently, the testimony of a witness swearing to facts which make against that side to which his passions evidently incline him, is entitled to the greatest weight. For this reason, the testimony of a person who voluntarily offers himself to be an evidence is always suspicious, or arguing a strong bias of passion or of interest.

Even the countenance, looks, and gestures of a witness, add to or take away from the weight of his testimony. It is therefore necessary, that those ex-

CHAP. V.

ternal criterions of veracity should not only be carefully attended to, but should be guarded, pure, and free from every endeavor of parties to interest, to warp, disguise, or suspect them. Hence all attempts to browbeat, perplex, or irritate a witness in the delivery of his testimony, are most reprehensible; and a court is not only deficient in a proper feeling of its own dignity, but positively in its bounden duty, if it do not repress such conduct with exemplary severity. As all attempts of this kind effect the weight of the evidence, they are in fact nearly allied to the punishable crime of subornation of perjury.

It is an idle question, which has been disputed by many writers on evidence, whether the greater weight is to be given to *written* testimony, or to that which is delivered *viva voce* upon oath by a witness? The question admits of no general answer; for the superior weight of either mode of proof depends upon the nature of the fact or matter at issue. Thus, if the point at issue were, whether A. were a member of a certain corporation, the written records of the corporation would be preferable evidence to the testimony of witness' swearing at his election on such a-day, or the contrary. But if the question were, whether A. did not stab B. with a sword on such a-day, and in such a place, the testimony of witnesses present at the rencounter would outweigh any written evidence brought to prove that A. was in a different place at the time: as the minutes of a society of which he was a member, the date of a letter from him bearing to be written from another place, &c. &c. In both these cases the weight is given to that species of testimony which is *the least liable to error or corruption.* In many cases, the evidence is compounded of both species of proof; and as the one sometimes encounters the other, it is necessary to adapt this principle, of determining to which of the two we ought to give the greatest weight.

CHAP. V.

OF VIVA VOCE, OR PAROLE-EVIDENCE.

Who may be witnesses.

THE law holds, that all persons who appear to have sufficient wisdom and discernment, and who, from their general character, are presumed to have a proper sense of the sacred obligation of an oath, are capable of being witnesses in a court of justice. Hence it follows, that when those essential requisites are found, and the witness understands, or can be made to understand the subject to which his testimony is required, and feels his obligation to speak the truth, it matters not of what country he is, or what language he speaks, (if his meaning can be conveyed to the court;) nor of what age he is; nor of what religion; provided he acknowledge a God, and be willing to bind himself by the requisite solemnity of an oath.

Persons excluded from giving testimony.

But the law positively excludes certain persons from giving testimony in a court of justice; and these may be reduced to four classes. 1. Those who have an interest in the matters at issue. 2. Those who stand in a certain relation to the parties in the cause. 3. Those who have committed crimes which destroy their credibily, or who are stigmatized by law. 4. Those who want sufficient discernment and understanding.

1. Of those disqualified through interest in the cause, the chief is the party, either prosecutor or defendant who cannot be allowed to give evidence for himself; but he is the best witness that can be against himself. But this rule is to be understood only of those who are to make actual gain, or suffer loss by the issue of the suit; for in many cases of a criminal nature, and when the object is not gain, or the avoidance of loss, but the punishment of a crime, the informer or prosecutor is allowed to give evidence against the party accused: one principal reason for such practice being the necessity of circumstances; for otherwise, many crimes would escape punishment for the want of evidence. Thus, in criminal courts, the party who suffers a

CHAP. V.

robbery, a rape, or an assault, is allowed to give evidence thereof against the offender; and in trials before courts-martial, a private party who is accuser, and who sustains the character of prosecutor jointly with the Judge-Advocate, may offer his own evidence upon oath in support of the charges. The court cannot refuse such testimony; but, as in all cases the jurors weigh their evidence, they will give to it the degree of credit only to which they conceive it is entitled. In all cases, the prosecutor may be called upon to give evidence in favor of the prisoner, or to produce records, or papers of any kind, which may be necessary for the prisoner's defence.* The informer on a penal statute, who,

* It was decided on the trial of the Hon. Lieut. Gen. James Murray, governor of Minorca, that the accuser and prosecutor is entitled to give his own evidence in support of any of the charges; and accordingly Sir Wm. Draper, who stood in that character upon the trial, gave evidence upon oath touching one of the charges which accused General Murray of personal wrong and injustice to him (Sir Wm. Draper). So likewise on the trial of Major Ingersol of the U. S. Regiment of Artillery, Lieut. Charles Woolstonecraft,

by law, is entitled to a part of the penalty, having a pecuniary interest in the suit, cannot be allowed to give testimony; though to this rule there are some exceptions, by particular and express enactment of the statute.

That is equally an interest which exempts from loss, and which entitles to gain. Those who have given bail cannot therefore be witnesses for their principal. On the same principle, the master of a ship being prosecuted for running over and sinking a barge, the evidence of a pilot was rejected, because he was answerable, if faulty in steering, to the master. But the law holds, that the gain or loss must be immediate and certain, and not contingent or barely possible. So it has been adjudged that an *heir apparent* might be a witness to prove the titles of lands, but a *remainder-man* could not.

who was accusor and prosecutor, gave his own evidence at length in support of the charges; and the practice is very common both in Europe and in this country.

CHAP. V.

Yet if the gain, though immediate, is such as cannot be supposed to influence any man of honorable principles to swear contrary to the truth, or even to give a biassed testimony, a court of justice will not repudiate his evidence. Thus the steward of a manor was admitted to prove, that by the custom of the manor, certain fines were due on the death of the lord to his heir, by the tenants, who were then readmitted, notwithstanding it was objected that the steward had fees on the readmission. On the same principle, in courts-martial, inferior officers who may gain promotion or rank by the conviction of their superiors, are not on that account excluded from giving testimony against them.

It has been adjudged, that the interest which amounts to a disqualification must be the obtaining of some actual profit bettering the witness' estate, or the immediate prospect of such profit; not the interest of establishing a higher character, or exculpating himself from a charge of misconduct or neglect.* But this distinction has no foundation in reason or good sense; for a man's character and reputation for good conduct, is his most valuable estate; and to protect these from injury is his dearest interest; which therefore must give the strongest bias to his testimony in every case, where these are concerned.

The judges of the court and the jurors† may be sworn as witnesses for any of the parties; for they have no interest in the issue of the trial, and no bias of any kind to give evidence against the truth.

A person who either receives or has been promised a pecuniary reward, or a benefit of any kind whatever to himself, to his family, or friends, or who receives or is promised the release of any obligation by the party who calls for his testimony, is disqualified on account of his interest in the suit.

* Espinasse on Nisi Prius, page 707.

† Hawkins' P. C. 432. Bacon's Abr. vol. 2. p. 286.

CHAP. V.

A person who has been threatened with vengeance of any kind, or any manner of mischief to himself, if he should refuse to give evidence in a certain way, is an incompetent witness for the party who has so threatened him. And reason urges, that his testimony *against* that party, though not absolutely inadmissible, is yet very suspicious, from the obvious motives of venum and malice.

A person cited as a witness for a defendant, is rejected on account of interest, if he be either a party in a similar cause actually in dependence, or is liable to prosecution on the same grounds, or for the same offence; for he is evidently prompted by interest to swear favorably for the defendant, that his acquittal may rule his own case.

The necessity of circumstances requires in many cases, that the evidence of interested persons should be admitted: As for example, in occult crimes, or where there is no penury of evidence. Thus, as before observed, the person who is robbed, ravished, or assaulted and beaten, is not disqualified from giving evidence; for otherwise, the criminal might often escape detection and punishment. But such evidence is always of a suspicious nature, and is not *per se* sufficient for conviction. On the same ground, the testimony of an accomplice, or *socius criminis*, who is pardoned, must often be resorted to for the discovery and punishment of crimes; but it will, in no case, merit the same weight with that of an unprejudiced and impartial witness.

In many cases the disqualification of interested persons is taken off by special statute. For the necessity of circumstances often requires their testimony.

For the same reason of necessity, it is adjudged, that where it is apparent that a statute law could receive no execution unless a party interested were to be admitted as a witness, there he must be allowed; for the law must not be rendered ineffectual by the impossibility

CHAP. V.

of proof.* The statute in this case may be said to abrogate the common law for just and necessary purpose, and in general when that purpose is apparent, and the circumstances of the case are such, as absolutely to require the evidence of parties interested, for the detection and punishment of a crime, then such witnesses must be admitted; the court and jury giving to their testimony such credibility as they judge it to deserve.

It has been already said, that the confession of a party, of the crime for which he is tried, is conclusive evidence against himself.

Persons relative to the parties.

2. Those who stand in a certain relation to the parties in the cause are disqualified from giving evidence.

The strongest of those disqualifying relations, is that of husband and wife; for these being in the eye of the law, but one person, it were the same as a party giving evidence in his own cause; besides, they are presumed to be

* Gibert's Law of Evidence, 4 edit. page 128.

CHAP. V.

under the strongest bias of affection and influence; and even where that presumption is manifestly excluded, the departure from this rule would lay the foundation of rancour and family disquiet, and so be hostile to the sacred institution of marriage. Husbands and wives, therefore, can neither be witnesses *for* or *against* each other in any action.

This rule applies, however, only where one of the married persons is a *party* in the action: For the wife may lawfully give evidence in a suit or trial between other persons, of which the issue may be contingently beneficial, or disadvantageous to her husband, and *vice versa*: Though the credit of such testimony must of course be suspicious.

It has been adjudged in some cases, that a husband and wife may be witnesses against one another in trials for treason; but the contrary has been likewise found and seems to be the better judgment.*

* Bacon's Abridgment, vol. 2, page 286.

CHAP. V.

It is generally held to be law, that no other relation of kindred, but that of husband and wife is excluded from giving evidence; and therefore, that parents may be witnesses for and against their children and *vice versa;* and children of the same parents for and against each other. But this doctrine is repugnant to the principle and foundation of evidence; for such testimony, *per se* is not sufficient to produce belief or conviction in any matter of doubt, or of material interest, there being such strong motives of favour and partiality. If the law, therefore, does not absolutely reject such testimony, the court or jury will receive it under all its circumstances of suspicion, and give it no more weight than it is entitled to. The Roman law, with more wisdom than ours, held such evidence altogether inadmissible.

Servants.

A servant in the cause of his master, though not attached to his person or household, is yet a suspected witness.

CHAP. V.

Counsel and Attornies.

Counsel and attornies, or solicitors, cannot in any case be called upon to give evidence, which may disclose the private business or secrets of their clients; but as the evidence of a necessary or important witness, might thus be taken off by giving him a fee, it is now understood to be the rule, that a counsel or attorney must be asked the previous question, whether he possesses the fact of his own knowledge, and previous to the retainer, or has learnt it from his client; and the witness will give his answer agreeable to the distinction. For example, supposing the question were concerning a rasure of a deed, or writing of any kind, he may be asked the question, whether he ever saw such deed or writing in a different plight? for that is a fact which he possesses of his own knowledge; but he must not be examined as to any confessions which his client might have made to him respecting it.* So he may be examined

* Lord Say's and Sele's case. Mic. 10, Ann.

CHAP. V.

as to the true time of the execution of a deed, or whether he saw a party sign.

On the same principle attornies and counsel are not obliged to produce papers, which may have been delivered to them by their client, as evidence against him. Thus an attorney being subpœnaed, and called to produce certain vouchers, which were to found a prosecution for forgery against his client, was found not obliged to obey the subpœna.

But this privilege is strictly confined to attornies and counsel acting in the cause, and cannot be extended to others, though professionally and confidentially employed. Nor is it extended to persons of other professions, though confidentially trusted by a party in a cause.

Those who are infamous on account of crimes, or stigmatized by the law.

3. Those who have committed crimes which destroy their credibility, are excluded from giving testimony in a court, as are also certain classes of persons stigmatized by the law.

The crimes which are held to destroy the credit of testimony, are felony, and the *crimen falsi*, as perjury and forgery; because these crimes destroy a man's moral reputation, and are understood to be the result of such wickedness and depravity as would render void the obligation of an oath; and to these is added treason, on account of the atrocity and danger of the crime, which it is expedient, by every means, to stigmatize and render odious. So likewise a person convicted of a conspiracy is an inadmissible witness.

Persons convicted of felony or of perjury, though pardoned, cannot be received as witnesses; for the pardon, though it remit the punishment, cannot wash out their moral turpitude. But a person convicted of treason, and pardoned, may be considered as restored to his reputation; for his crime is presumed to have arisen from an error in judgment, and the receiving of a pardon is held to be a pledge of his future allegiance.

It is the commission of the crime and not the nature of the punishment, nor the suffering of that punishment, which makes the party infamous. Thus the commission of the crime of farratry, or

CHAP. V.

the stirring up of law-suits, a crime of a nature equally infamous and pernicious, has been adjudged to render the perpetrator incapable of giving evidence, though the punishment was only a fine. Yet it may be questioned, whether a punishment of a disgraceful and infamous nature, having an effect of debasing the character and destroying the reputation of the sufferer, ought not to incapacitate from giving testimony; as for example, standing in the pillory, whipping, if inflicted by the sentence of a criminal court, &c. As whipping, however, is a military punishment, which is often inflicted for small failures in duty, and is to be looked upon rather in the light of a wholesome chastisement than an infamous punishment, it ought not to render a soldier an incompetent evidence; though according to the nature of the offence for which it has been inflicted, it may affect the credit of his testimony.

A conviction for perjury, even tho' followed by a pardon, ought forever to incapacitate the convict from giving evidence, because he has furnished demonstrative proof, that he is insensible to the sacred bond of an oath.*

It has been already observed, that the testimony of an accomplice or *particeps criminis*, is in many cases to be received, from the necessity of circumstances, but he is never entitled to the credit of an unsuspected witness.

In all cases where a party would avail himself of the incompetency of a witness on occount of his conviction of a crime, it is necessary that he should produce to the court the record of conviction, or a sufficient proof of it.

No witness is obliged to answer any question, the answer to which may oblige him to accuse himself of any crime or punishable offence. But it has been

* It is a most absurd distinction which has been drawn by some writers on evidence, and even confirmed by the judgments of the courts, that "on perjury "at common law, the party pardoned may be a witness "because the king has the power to take off every part "of the penalty, and so discern whether it is fit the offender should be restored to credibility; but if a man "be indicted for perjury on the statute, the king's par-"don cannot restore his credibility."

CHAP. V.

adjudged, that a witness was obliged to answer the question, whether he had ever stood in the pillory? for the answer could not subject him to a new punishment.*

There are certain classes of persons whom the law stigmatizes, and declares incapable of bearing evidence, though not convicted of any crime.

As the sanction of an oath depends upon the belief of a God, it can have no obligation on those persons who openly deny the being or attributes of the Deity. Professed atheists from principle, therefore, and those who from ignorance or babarism have no impressions of religion, are justly declared incapable of giving testimony upon oath.

But it is not necessary that a witness should profess the Christian religion. Jews are competent witnesses, as are Mahometans; the former being sworn upon the *Old Testament*, and the latter upon the *Koran*. So likewise persons of any other religion provided

* Rex. v. Edwards, 4. Term Rep. 440.

CHAP. V.

they swear or affirm by Almighty God, that they will tell the truth and the whole truth. There is no particular form essential to the oath to be taken by a witness. "As the purpose of an "oath," says Lord Mansfield, "is to "bind the conscience, every man of "every religion should be bound by "that form which he himself thinks "will bind his conscience most."* So Gentoos have been sworn according to the ceremonies of their religion, and admitted as good witnesses.

Quakers.

Quakers, whose religious tenets debar the taking of an oath, are allowed to give evidence upon their simple affirmation. "I do solemnly, sincerely, "and truly affirm."

Persons who want discernment or understanding.

4. Those persons who want sufficient discernment and understanding, are inadmissible as witnesses.

Infants, and children of tender age, are excluded from giving testimony, on account of defect of understanding; but as the opening and growth of the un-

* Atcheson v. Everalt. Cowp. 382. Hill.

derstanding is various in different individuals, the law has fixed no determinate age for their admissibility as witnesses. A child of nine years of age has been allowed to give evidence; but the credit to be given to such testimony must always rest with the court and jurors.

Idiots or insane persons are utterly incapable of giving evidence; though lunatics, and those subject to temporary fits of insanity, may be received in their lucid intervals. Mere weakness of understanding does not render a witness incompetent, though it may discredit his evidence. Persons deaf and dumb from their birth may be admitted as witnesses, provided they are capable of distinct information by means of arbitrary signs, clearly and unequivocally to express their knowledge of facts, or make their testimony plainly intelligible to a court; and provided, likewise, they can give clear intimation that they understand the moral and religious nature of an oath.

OF WRITTEN EVIDENCE.

WRITTEN evidence is of two kinds; public and private. Public is, 1. records or memorials of the legislature, and of the courts of justice; 2. public matters of inferior nature. Records are either acts of congress, or authenticated proceedings of the courts of record. All of which it is evident must give the greatest faith, and be received as complete proof, in any court, of the facts or matters which they contain. But as the original records themselves cannot be transferred from place to place, for private purposes, authenticated copies of these proceedings or records must be allowed in evidence. Thus the printed statute book is held to be an authenticated copy of all public or general acts of the legislature, and must be received as good evidence; but private acts are not to be received on the evidence of the statute book, they must be compared with the record. A copy

Public written evidence.

CHAP. V.

of a copy is no evidence at all. The proceedings of the courts of record, which are admitted as good evidence, are judgments of those courts and verdicts of juries, authenticated either under the proper seal, or sworn copies; that is, such as the producer swears he examined with the original, as the copy of a judgment from New-Hampshire, produced in a court in Georgia. Such records are evidences of the highest nature, and are conclusive proof of the matters which they contain.

Public matters of inferior nature which are not recorded, but which are admitted as written evidence in courts of justice, are bills and answers in chancery; depositions or testimonies given in writing, when the witness who made them is dead, or cannot be procured; for if he be alive, and can be produced to the court, so as to be cross-examined, the deposition must be rejected, as not being the best evidence that can be had. The register of baptisms, marriages and burials, or an authenticated copy from it, is good evidence; and in general it is held that all books of that public nature, are sufficient evidence of the matters of which they are the proper registers. Depositions given by a witness on a former trial, cannot be received as evidence on another trial, unless the evidence has died in the interim. But depositions given upon a former trial, or before a magistrate, may be read at a trial, in order to take off the credit of a witness, by shewing a variation in his testimony. The examination of an informer, taken upon oath, and subscribed by him before a magistrate, cannot be received as evidence upon the trial, unless it be proved on oath, that the informer is dead, or is unable, through sickness, to attend the court, or is kept away by procurement of the prisoner. It is not sufficient to prove that the prosecutors used their utmost endeavours to find him, without effect.

Private written evidence may be, books of accounts, either of parties, or of their persons, receipts, discharges, bills of parcels, gazettes, or news-pa-

CHAP. V.

pêrs, notes of hand, and bill of exchange, letters of correspondence, &c. The persuasion of the veracity of a merchant's books, arises from their regularity. If that regulartiy therefore, be wanting, they ought to give no faith in judgment. At best, however, they are incomplete evidence, *per se*, in favour of the merchant or person who keeps them; but they are good evidence against him. Letters of correspondence and all familiar writings, must be authenticated, that is, proved upon oath to be written by the person of whose hand writing they are alleged to be. The comparison of hand-writings, tho' it may usefully be employed in the detection of forgery, is no evidence to authenticate any writing whatever as a piece of testimony. It may, however, furnish a presumption which will weigh in the scale with other evidence.

CHAP. V.

OF PROBABILITY, AND THE WEIGHING OF EVIDENCE.

A THING is probable in proportion, as it agrees with what usually happens in similar circumstances. It is natural that the mind should more easily give its faith to things which are probable from most usually happening, than to matters that are repugnant to that probability; and therefore, in judicial proceedings a much smaller degree of evidence ought to be held sufficient to establish the truth of the former, than it required to prove the latter. A single witness may be sufficient evidence of a probable fact, whereas, it may require the concurring testimony of many to prove what is not likely to have happened in such and such circumstances. In criminal matters, it is often difficult to say whether the *probability* is for guilt or innocence; but the law with great humanity holds, that the *presumption* should always be in favour of innocence, and that no person should be convicted of a crime unless upon the strongest and most satisfactory evidence. Positive proof therefore, is always to be required where it can be had; as the testimony of two or more impartial witnesses swearing directly to the facts. Where a proof of this kind is wanting, circumstantial and presumptive evidence must be resorted to, that is, a proof of a number of concurring circumstances, which usually attend certain facts, and which may furnish such strong motives of belief of the facts themselves, as nothing but a positive proof to the contrary can destroy. As if A. and B. two persons who were known to be at mortal enmity with each other, or between whom it was known that a challenge had passed, should be observed to walk out together to a private place, armed with swords, and be seen by a passenger engaged in actual combat, and A. should be found dead, and B. seen coming from the place with his sword bloody, or marks of blood upon his clothes. These are violent presumptions, and create a belief, which nothing but positive proof could destroy; as for example, the confession of C. that he had interfered between the parties when fighting, and in order to save the life of his friend B. had himself put A. to death.

The credibility of a witness, is what alone gives weight to his evidence, and in judging of his credibility, many considerations must enter into the account: as condition and rank in life, general reputation, known principles, judgment and good sense, accuracy of memory, perfect indifference to the matters in issue, and freedom from prejudice and partiality.

An unwilling and reluctant witness, who speaks with caution, answering nothing but what is forced out of him by repeated and circuitous interrogation, is unworthy of the same credit that is given to one who openly and fairly declares all that he knows upon the point. On the other hand, a witness who amplifies in his testimony, unnecessarily enlarging upon circumstances unfavorable to a party, who seems to be gratifyed by the opportunity of furnishing condem-

CHAP. V.

natory evidence, or manifestly betrays passion and prejudice in the substance of his testimony, or in the manner of delivering it, is to be listened to with equal suspicion of his veracity.

If a witness takes upon himself to remember with the greatest minuteness, all the circumstances of transactions long since past, and which are of a frivolous nature, and not likely to dwell in the memory, his testimony is thereby rendered very suspicious; as, on the other hand, a witness affirming his total want of recollection of the most material and striking circumstances of a recent and remarkable fact, which happened in his own presence, is deserving of very little credit in those particulars which he pretends to remember.

In all cases, however, the discerning mind of a juror will be at no loss to separate the truth of an evidence from its falsehood; and where the former reluctantly breaks forth, he will give it the greater credit, as being the testimony of conscience, not only unin-

CHAP. V.

fluenced by the passions, but directly against their perverting influence.

A single witness requires much corroboration from concurring circumstances; for where there is no presumption from circumstances fortifying his evidence, the credit of that person would need to be very high indeed, whose single and unsupported testimony should give faith to any criminal accusation.

Witnesses should always show the causes of their knowledge, for the weight of the testimony must be in proportion to the opportunity which the witness had of knowing the facts. If, therefore, a man cannot set forth a probable cause of knowledge, he is not to be believed at all.

A single witness, &c.

The attestation of a witness must be only to what he actually knows from his own observation of the facts in issue. He is not to be examined as to what he has heard, or been informed of by others; for his testimony being in that case a reference to the information of another who is not upon oath, is no evidence at all. Yet a witness may swear to a re-

CHAP. V.

port, or that so and so, other persons have said, (for it may be material to prove that there was such a report), though he can give no evidence to the truth of the matters reported. So likewise, though hearsay is no direct evidence of the truth of the things said, or related, yet it may be brought collaterally in support of a witness' testimony; as if a person would swear that he heard the witness frequently tell the story which he has now given upon oath, to various persons at the time, and with the same circumstances; or it may be brought to discredit that testimony, by proving that the witness said directly otherwise to many persons at the time.

Questions of opinion.

In general, facts are the only subject of evidence, and not opinions; for it is perhaps only of matters of fact that there can be absolute certainty or truth: Facts are positive, determinate, and immutable; but opinions are not only various but mutable. It is therefore only to the truth of *facts* that evidence is regularly brought; and to form *opinions* on these, is the province, not of the witness, but of the judge or juror who is to decide upon them. No party therefore in a trial is entitled to obtrude the opinions of a witness upon the court or jury, or to call upon a witness to answer questions of opinion. Yet there are cases in which a juror may desire the opinion of a witness on certain points, in order to regulate his own final judgment or verdict; and the court, if it sees the propriety of that desire, will call upon the witness to give his opinion. This has frequently occurred upon courts-martial;* and there are indeed certain Articles of War, upon which if a person is to be tried, there is a strict propriety, and even necessity, for the witnesses answering questions of opinion: as for example, if an officer is arraigned under that Article of War which punishes with dismissal from the service all such scandalous or infamous behaviour as is unbecoming an officer and a gentleman, it is obvious, that it may be in such a case absolutely neces-

* The trial of lord George Sackville.

CHAP. V.

sary to make a witness declare his opinion of the prisoner's conduct. So likewise, if an officer is accused of behaving with contempt or disrespect to his general or commanding officer, of being found drunk on duty, of quitting his division or post without necessity, &c. All these are cases in which opinion is so combined with fact, that it is either impossible that they should be separated in a witness' testimony, or unfit that they should be so: but, as already said, the court is, in all questions of this nature, to determine as to the propriety of questions of opinion being put and answered. With regard to the questions of doubtful propriety, the best rule that can be followed is, that every thing which, on the part of the prosecutor, tends to support or give credibility to the charges, is admissible evidence; as is likewise, on the part of the prisoner, every thing that has a tendency to invalidate or discredit them; though in both cases the tendency in either way should be but remote.

It frequently happens, that the tentency of a question put to a witness may be to the prejudice of a third person, who is no party to the trial. This consequence ought in justice and humanity to be avoided whenever it is possible; and in no case ought the *prosecutor* to be allowed this liberty of indirectly impeaching or affecting the characters of third parties; because it cannot be necessary to his purpose, but it may sometimes happen that the *party accused* may find it absolutely necessary in defence of himself, to throw blame, and even criminality on others who are no parties to the trial: Nor can a prisoner be refused that liberty, which is essential to his own justification. It is sufficient for the party aggrieved, that the law can furnish ample redress against all calumnies or unjust accusations.

Witness may be called to support the credibility of witnesses, either by giving testimony to their general good character, or to their knowledge or acquaintance with the facts in issue, or to

CHAP. V.

their having invariably related facts in the same manner.

If, therefore, the credibility of any of the witnesses, either for the prosecutor or prisoner, is impeached by the opposite party, it becomes proper to re-establish their credibility, by examining new evidences thereto.

HOW WITNESSES ARE TO BE SUMMONED, AND MANNER OF GIVING THEIR EVIDENCE.

ALL military persons are bound by their duty to attend and furnish testimony in all military courts, whenever required so to do by a proper authority. This authority is contained in the warrant, or order for assembling the court-martial; and in consequence thereof, the prosecutor and prisoner must, respectively summon, or give warning to those persons who are necessary evidence, of the time and place of meeting of the court, and make requisitions for their compliance to give testimony.

In general, military persons are not allowed any sum, in the name of charges or expenses, for their attendance upon a court-martial; because such service is held to be a part of their professional duty. Yet, the law provides an allowance in cases wherein they are obliged to incur expenses in travelling to and from general courts-martial, and while sitting, as a member, or attending as a witness. But a witness in a civil line of life is by law entitled to all their reasonable expenses.

All witnesses must be regularly sworn, in presence of the court and of the parties, and give their testimony likewise in their presence. In courts-martial, the testimony of the witness is to be taken down in writing, as nearly as possible in his own words, and read to him for his approval or correction, after his testimony is closed.

In case a material witness should be confined to his room by sickness, so as to prevent his appearance before the

CHAP. V.

court, the only correct method of obtaining his testimony, is for the court to adjourn to the house and bed chamber of the sick person, and there take down his evidence in the usual form, or if that cannot be done, by the Judge-Advocate and the prisoner writing their interrogatories and cross-interrogatories, and by a magistrate's receiving the answers of the witness on oath, and certifying them to the court. But this last method ought not to be practised in a capital case.

All objections to the competency of a witness must be stated in open court; but as a court-martial never deliberates with open doors, the court must be cleared in order to weigh the import of the objection, and when the court have come to a resolution, it is afterwards communicated in open court to all parties.

Perjury.

A witness before a court-martial gives his testimony under the solemnity of an oath.

If, therefore, a wilful perjury is committed in his testimony, by a person subject to the military law, there is no doubt that a court-martial, by their own power, can immediately inflict such discretionary punishment on the offender, as they may judge suitable to the offence. If the perjury is committed by a person not under military authority, but who is brought to give evidence in a court-martial, the court will direct the party injured, or the Judge-Advocate, as public prosecutor, to prosecute the offender in the proper civil court.

Subornation of perjury.

Subornation of perjury, or the procuring of witnesses to swear falsely, stands on the same footing with perjury.

CHAPTER VI.

Of the Judgment of a Court-Martial.

THE last stage of the trial before a court-martial, is the exercise by the court of its judicial functions, in the return of a solemn verdict on the guilt or innocence of the prisoner, and pronouncing sentence; and this is to be done with closed doors, after the parties, and all indifferent persons have been ordered to withdraw.

The proceedings must be read over to the court.

As the court is now in possession of the whole evidence, which has been carefully reduced into writing, by the Judge-Advocate, as recorder of the court, together with all arguments upon the evidence, both on the part of the prosecutor and prisoner, it is customary before proceeding to deliberate upon the judgment, that the court should hear the proceedings read over by the Judge-Advocate, which answers the double purpose of bringing the whole body of the evidence into one connected view, to the recollection of the members, and ascertaining the accuracy and fidelity of the record, by comparing it with the notes taken by individual members, in the course of the trial.

In complicated cases, in circumstantial proofs, in cases where a number of prisoners are jointly arraigned, as on charges of mutiny, or the like, it is expedient that the Judge-Advocate should arrange and methodise the body of the evidence, applying it distinctly to the facts of the charge, and bringing home to each prisoner, where there are more than one, the result of the proof against him, balanced with the evidence of exculpation or alleviation. In ordinary cases, a charge of this kind from the Judge-Advocate, is not so necessary.

Deliberation and judgment of the court.

When there are distinct and separate charges, or articles of accusation, the president and members of the court reason and deliberate separately on each charge; candidly discussing, in a free and open conversation, the import

CHAP. VI.

of the evidence, and allowing its full weight to every argument or presumption in favour of the prisoner, and being thus ripe for the decision, the Judge-Advocate puts the question of "guilty, or not guilty of the charge," to each of the members, beginning with the youngest,* and so, progressively, up to the president, and writing down from each member, his vote and opinion, for acquittal or conviction. The votes are then counted, and if the majority declare the prisoner *not guilty*, he is accordingly acquitted. If, on the other hand, the majority declare the prisoner *guilty*, the court proceeds next to determine what punishment shall be awarded, and to pronounce their sentence for its infliction. The opinion or votes of the members are taken in this last question in the same manner as on the former; nor are those members who have in the previous question voted for acquittal, to be debarred from voting on the second, which is to decide the de-

* Article of War, 72.

gree or nature of the punishment; for it would be most unjust that those who thought so favourably of the prisoner's case as to vote for absolute acquittal, should, from that circumstance, be precluded from rendering the punishment as mild as possible. The punishments which it is in the power of a court-martial to inflict, are various in their nature and degree, from the highest, which is *death*, down to those of the lightest nature, as a short confinement for a private soldier, or a reprimand for a commissioned officer. It is humanely provided by the Articles of War, that no sentence of death shall be pronounced against any offender, unless two-thirds of the members shall concur in the sentence. In some particular cases, the Articles of War point out the express punishment to be awarded in consequence of certain acts; as thus, "Every officer who shall be convicted before a general court-martial, of having signed a false certificate, relating to the absence of either officer or private soldier, or relative to his or their pay,

Military punishments.

CHAP. VI.

shall be cashiered."* So likewise in the case of an officer knowingly receiving a deserter from any other corps, without confining him and giving notice to the regiment to which he formerly belonged.†

In such cases the court has no discretionary powers, but must pronounce the sentence which the law requires, whenever the fact is proved. There are but two instances in which capital sentences are decreed by the Articles of War, without a discretionary power of the court of commuting the punishment. The one is contained in the 55th Article of War—" Whosoever be-" longing to the armies of the United " States employed in foreign parts, shall " force a safe-guard, shall suffer death." The other is the 2nd Section, concerning spies, where it is enacted, " That " in time of war, all persons not citi-" zens of, or owing allegiance to the " United States of America, who shall " be found lurking as spies, in or about

* Article of War 14. † Article of War 22.

CHAP. VI.

" the fortifications or encampments of " the armies of the United States, or " any of them, shall suffer death, ac- " cording to law and the usage of na- " tions, by sentence of a general court- " martial." In crimes of a less atrocious nature, the Articles of War declare simply, that the offender shall be punished at the discretion of a general court-martial; omitting the word *death*, which evidently implies, that the power of punishing capitally is excluded in such cases, indeed it is positively declared so by the 87th Article of War. The inferior punishments are various, according to the degree of the crimes, and rank of the persons who commit them.

Cashiering.

Of those peculiar to the rank of commissioned officers, the most severe of the inferior punishments is *cashiering*, that is, depriving an officer of his commission, breaking him, by taking from him the honorable character of a soldier, and reducing him to the station of a private citizen. This is sometimes done *simply*, that is, without carrying in the sentence and judgment against

CHAP. VI.

the offender of incapacity to be restored afterwards to his military character; or with the addition of a judgment of a court, declaring the offender "utterly "unfit or disabled to have or to hold "any office or employment in the ser- "vice of the United States;"* which is the highest of the subordinate punishments that can be inflicted on a commissioned officer.

Suspension.

2. Suspension from rank and pay, which deprives an officer of his military character, and suspends his functions and emoluments for a definite period of time, viz. a year, six months, or three months from the date of the sentence, according to the culpability of the officer.

Reprimand.

3. Reprimand, public or private. A public reprimand is inflicted by the officer approving the sentence of the court-martial, or by the commanding officer of the regiment or garrison to which the party may belong, according to the term of the sentence, and on which occasion

* Articles of War 15 & 16

the troops are paraded to hear it. The severity of the reprimand is not prescribed by the sentence, but is left to the discretion of the commander in chief, by whose authority the sentence is put into execution, and it must be regulated according to circumstances and the degree of the offence. A private reprimand is given by the commanding officer to the party without the presence of witnesses.

The inferior punishments peculiar to the state of non-commissioned officers and soldiers, are corporal punishments; as whipping, imprisonment, &c. In cases of desertion, when a court-martial may not think the offence deserving of capital punishment, they often adjudge the offender to serve at hard labor in some of the fortifications during the remainder of his term of service.*

* This mode of punishing deserters in time of peace, was particularly recommended by the late Major General Hamilton, while Commander in Chief, of the Army of the United States.

CHAP. VI.

Reducing.

The Articles of War enact for certain offences, the reducing of non-commissioned officers to the station of private soldiers, as for crimes of embezzling money, &c. or conniving at one soldier's hiring another to do his duty, &c. This power of reducing non-commissioned officers to the station of a private sentinel, rests at all times with the commanding officer or colonel of the regiment or corps, and can be exercised by his own authority, on a sufficient cause, without the intervention of a court-martial; a discretionary power, which has furnished much topic for discussion, and frequent occasion of blame, but is founded on a just and necessary policy, and has never in practice been attended with improper consequences.

In general, the sentence of courts-martial declares the prisoner guilty or not of the special matters of the charge, and in the event of guilt, awards the proper punishment. But sometimes the degree of criminality actually proved against the prisoner, though of the same nature, may fall short in extent of the crime or accusation: as for example, the crime charged may be desertion, but the proof may amount to no more than absence without leave. In such case the court by its judgment ought to acquit from the charge of desertion, but find the prisoner guilty of the inferior offence and award a corresponding punishment. But although this rule ought to be followed where the offence proved is of the same nature, though less in degree than the crime contained in the charge, it will not hold good where the offence proved against the prisoner is either of a different nature altogether from that which is charged, or of a higher degree of criminality; for the court is not warranted to go beyond the indictment, nor has the prisoner received a fair or legal notice to prepare his defence against either a different crime, or a higher degree of guilt than is contained in the charges. If therefore evidence should emerge in the course of the trial, of greater criminality against the prisoner, or of his guilt of a sepa-

CHAP. VI.

rate crime, it is competent for the court, after exhausting the actual charges, by their proper sentence, to report their opinion to the commander by whose order the court is held, and to re-commit the party into confinement, in order that he may be brought to a new trial.

General observations on the form and nature of sentences of courts-martial.

The form of the sentence of the court-martial must vary according to the circumstances of the case on which it is pronounced; but a few general observations may here be made applicable to all sentences whatsoever of general courts-martial.

As to the tenor of the oath administered to all the members of the court, they are sworn, at no time whatsoever, nor upon any account, to discover or disclose the particular vote or opinion of any member, unless required to give evidence thereof in a court of justice in a due course of law;* so that it is evidently not proper that the sentence of the court-martial should express by what majority of the members it was

* Article of War 69.

pronounced; because that might lead to the discovery of particular votes or opinions; nor although the court is unanimous in its judgment, is it proper to express that circumstance in the sentence; for this in fact is disclosing the votes and opinions of all the members; yet there seems to be no impropriety if there should be an unanimous concurrence of the members for recommendation to the mercy of the President or commander in chief, that this circumstance should then be mentioned, as giving the greater weight to the application, and at the same time not leading to the discovery of particular opinions respecting the sentence itself by which the prisoner has been condemned.

The opinions and sentence of the court may be either general in their tenor, that is, declaring the prisoner *guilty* or *not guilty* of the articles of charge; or they may be special, finding certain parts *proved*, or *not proved;* in consequence of which, they declared him guilty, or not guilty, on those articles: for, in all cases, the guilt or inno-

CHAP. VI.

cence of the prisoner with respect to the particular charges, must be pointedly proved and declared; otherwise the court do not discharge the whole of their duty, which requires, that they should not only decide whether the facts are proved, or unproved, but likewise pronounce their judgment on the criminality of those facts.

It was formerly a very usual custom, to express in the sentence of courts-martial, the particular Articles of War, of which the sentence declared the prisoner to be guilty of a breach or violation; but the more recent, and better practice, is to omit all such reference to the Articles of War; as being in itself unnecessary and frequently affording handle for cavilling, and sophistical objections of irregularity, or incongruity with the articles referred to. If the sentence should be called in question, as not warranted by any positive Article of the Military Law, it is the province of the party who then arraigns the judgment, to prove his objection, by pointing out that incongruity; for the presumption is, that the decree and judgment of all courts are warranted by law.*

For a reason nearly allied to the above, it would seem most adviseable for courts-martial in their opinions and sentences, to avoid all unnecessary minuteness, in detailing and specifying the grounds of those opinions and judgments, and in particular to avoid all arguments in justification of their sentences; for it is unwise in any court to hold forth to the public a challenge to impugn their judgment, or purposely to invite to a discussion of the grounds on which they have proceeded. If a sentence be general and without any assignment of special reasons, it may be defended by all good reasons which are applicable to the matter; but if it assign its special grounds, it must stand or fall by those alone.

* Lord Mansfield has observed, that the decrees of governors in the West-Indies, acting as chancellors, were always right in honesty and common sense, but not being lawyers, they always erred in attempting to give legal reasons for their decrees.

CHAP. VI.

It must at the same time be observed, that in cases of a circumstantial nature, and when the sentence of the court is not general upon the whole matters of charge, but special, finding the prisoner guilty of some points of accusation, and acquitting him of others; as the punishment to be awarded ought to be in strict proportion to the measure of guilt, so it may be extremely proper, in such cases, to specify in the sentence, the particular grounds of the opinion and judgment of the court.

CHAPTER VII.

Of Appeals from a Regimental or Garrison Court-Martial, to a General Court-Martial.

THE right of appeal from regimental or garrison courts-martial, seems to be authorised in one particular case only, which is, when an inferior officer or soldier shall think himself wronged by his captain or other officer.

It is declared by 35th Article of War, that such officer or soldier, who shall think himself wronged, is to complain thereof to the commanding officer of the regiment, who is thereby required to summons a regimental court-martial, for the doing justice to the complainant, from which regimental court-martial, either party may, if he thinks himself still aggrieved, appeal to a general court-martial. But if upon a second hearing, the appeal shall appear vexatious and groundless, the person so appealing,

CHAP. VII.

shall be punished at the discretion of said court-martial. It would hence appear, that in all such cases of alleged wrong or injustice, committed by superior officers towards their inferiors, the right of appeal cannot be refused, but must of course be granted, by the commander in chief's appointment of a general court-martial, to take cognizance of the cause. The only check against rash and ill-founded applications in the cases of the above nature, is the certainty that an adequate punishment will not fail to attend every unjust and groundless appeal.

The reason why a power of appeal is declared to be a matter of absolute right to inferior officers or soldiers, complaining of being wronged by their superior officers is, that a regimental or garrison court-martial has not the power of inflicting any punishment on commissioned officers: They can do no more than express their opinion, that the complaint is just, or the contrary, and where it is practicable and proper, relieve the sufferer as to any existing grievance; but the injury complained of, however flagrant, must therefore have remained unredressed, as far as punishment is conceived, if an appeal to a general court-martial had not been declared to be a matter of right to the party aggrieved.

CHAPTER VIII.

Of Courts of Inquiry.

Authority for holding courts of inquiry and their functions.

COURTS of Inquiry are held by the same authority as general or regimental courts-martial, and have power to examine witnesses on oath, and compel their attendance in the same manner, but they are intrusted with powers only "to examine into the nature of any "transaction, accusation or imputation "against any officer or soldier. But "they are not empowered to give their "opinion on the merits of the case, ex- "cepting they shall be thereunto spe- "cially required."

Members of the Court.

Courts of inquiry may consist of one or more officers, not exceeding three and a Judge-Advocate, or other suitable person, as a Recorder, to reduce the proceedings and evidence to writing, and all of whom must be sworn to the faithful performance of their duty.

CHAP. VIII.

Form of Proceeding.

The form of proceeding in courts of inquiry is nearly the same as that in courts-martial. The members being assembled, the Judge-Advocate or Recorder administers the members the following oath: "You shall well and "truly examine and inquire, according "to your evidence, into the matter now "before you, without partiality, favor, "affection, prejudice, or hope of reward: "*So help you God.*" After which the President administers to the Judge-Advocate or Recorder, the following oath:

"You do swear, that you will, according to your best abilities, accurately and impartially record the proceedings of the court, and the evidence to be given in the case in hearing: *So help you God.*"

The accusation is then read, and the witnesses are examined by the court, and the parties accused are also permitted to cross-examine and interrogate the witnesses, so as to investigate fully the circumstances in question.*

* Article of War 91.

CHAP. VIII.

The examination of the witnesses having gone through with, the president orders the court to be cleared. The recorder then reads over the whole of the proceedings, as well for the purpose of correcting the record, as for aiding the memory of the members of the court. After mature deliberation on the evidence adduced, proceed to declare, whether or no the grounds of accusation are sufficient to bring the matter before a general court-martial, or to give their opinion of the merits of the case, if so required in the warrant issued for assembling the court.

The proceedings must be authenticated by the signatures of the Recorder and President.

The proceedings must be authenticated by the signature of the president, and delivered to the commanding officer; and the said proceedings may be admitted in evidence by a court-martial, in cases not capital, or extending to the dismission of an officer, provided oral testimony cannot be obtained. But the law declares, that as courts of inquiry may be diverted to dishonorable purposes, and may be considered as engines of destruction to military merit, in the

Courts of inquiry prohibited unless di-

CHAP. VIII.

rected by the President or demanded by the accused.

hands of weak and envious commandants, they are expressly prohibited, unless directed by the President of the United States, or demanded by the accused.*

It were to be wished that courts of inquiry were more frequently resorted to than is usually done, or rather that it were a matter of established usage, that no person should be put upon his trial before a general court-martial, unless by a previous report by an inquest, on evidence laid before them, that there appears sufficient grounds for calling the party to defend himself judicially against the matters of accusation. A preliminary form of this nature would be of infinite service in the repression of calumnious and frivolous prosecutions; and would tend more than any other measure to the checking of that extreme frequency of trials by courts-martial, which has the worst effect upon the public mind, reflecting dishonor on the military character in general, spread-

* Article of War 92.

CHAP. VIII.

ing disunion and party divisions among the members of a corps, and frequently laying the foundation of permanent and even fatal animosities.

In many cases, a court of inquiry acting as umpires or arbitrators between the parties, might compose differences or explain misunderstandings, so as to prevent the necessity of all further procedure, by actual arraignment and trial.

CHAPTER IX.

Of the Office and Duties of the Judge-Advocate.

Judge-Advocate prosecutes in the name of the U. S.

For sustaining the interest of the United States in trials before a general court-martial, an officer is appointed under the title of Judge-Advocate, to prosecute in their name; for as in all criminal trials, the State, whose laws are violated, is understood to be the party injured, and which is entitled to demand redress by the punishment of the guilty person, which function in the ordinary courts of law, is discharged by the Attorney-General: so in offences against the military law which are not cognizable by the ordinary tribunals, but are declared to be specially so by courts-martial, the Judge-Advocate is appointed to fulfil a similar duty, and to prosecute in the name of the United States all officers and soldiers, who shall be guilty of any breach of the military law, either as contained

CHAP. IX.

in the Articles of War, or other regulations issued for the government of the army.

His functions are various.

The appropriate functions of the Judge-Advocate, as an essential officer in all general courts-martial, are various in their nature, and as the Articles of War do not describe them with much precision, we are therefore obliged, in suppliment of what is found in that direct authority, to resort to the less positive, though equally binding authority of established usage and practice.

The Articles of War are silent on the subject of the Judge-Advocate assisting the court with his counsels and advice, as to any matters of form or law; it nevertheless is understood to be his duty to explain any doubts which may arise in the course of their deliberations, and prevent any irregularities or deviations from the regular form of proceeding. For it is to be observed, that in all matters touching the trials of crimes by courts-martial, wherever the Military Law is silent, the rules of the Common Law of the Land, to the benefit of which all citizens are entitled for the protection of life, liberty, and reputation, must of necessity be resorted to; and every material deviation from these rules, unless warranted by some express enactment of the military code, is, in fact, a punishable offence in the members of the court-martial. Hence arises the absolute necessity for some members of the court being conversant in the general doctrines of the law, in so far as they relate to the trials of crimes, and the weighing of evidence; and the person to whom the court is naturally to look for information of this kind, is the Judge-Advocate, who is either by profession a lawyer, or whose duty, if he be not professionally such, is to instruct himself in the common law and practice of the ordinary courts in the trial of crimes.

In the performance of this duty, the Judge-Advocate will always be guided by a just sense of his official character and situation. As he has no judicial power, nor any determinative voice, either in the sentence or interlocutory

CHAP. IX.

opinions of the court, so he is not entitled to regulate or direct those sentences or opinions, or in any other shape to interfere in the proceedings of the court, farther than by giving of counsel or advice; and his own discretion must be his sole director in suggesting when that may be seasonable, proper, or necessary. On every occasion when the court demands his opinion, he is bound to give it with freedom and amplitude; and even when not requested to deliver his sentiments, his duty requires that he should put the court upon their guard against every deviation, either from any essential or necessary forms in their proceedings, or a violation of justice in their final sentence and judgment. A remonstrance of this nature, urged with due deference and respect, will seldom, it is to be presumed, fail to meet with its proper regard from the court; but should it happen that an illegal measure, or an unjust opinion is nevertheless persevered in, the Judge-Advocate, though not warranted to enter his dissent in the form of a protest upon the record of the proceedings, (for that implies a judicative voice) ought to engross therein the opinion delivered by him upon the controverted point, in order not only that he may stand absolved from all imputation of failure in his duty of giving counsel, but that the error or wrong may be fairly brought under the consideration of that power with whom it lies, in the last resource, either to approve and order into effect, or to remit the operation of the sentence.

Another part of the official duty of the Judge-Advocate, which, though not enjoined by any particular enactment of the Military Law, has yet the sanction of general and established practice, is, that he should assist the prisoner in the conduct of his defence. This duty is more especially incumbent on the Judge-Advocate in cases where the prisoner has not the aid of professional counsel to direct him, which generally happens in the trials of private soldiers, who, wanting all advantages of education, or opportunities of mental improvement, must stand greatly in need

CHAP. IX.

of advice in such trying circumstances as are often sufficient to overwhelm the acutest intellect, and embarras or suspend the powers of the most cultivated understanding. It is certainly not to be understood, that in discharging this office, which is prescribed solely by justice and humanity, the Judge-Advocate should in the strictest sense, consider himself as bound to the duty of a counsel in exerting his ingenuity to defend the prisoner at all hazards, against those charges which, in his capacity of prosecutor, he is, on the other hand, bound to urge, and to sustain by proof; for understood to this extent, the one duty is utterly inconsistent and incompatible with the other. All that is required, is, that in the same manner as in the civil courts of criminal jurisdiction, the judges are understood to be counsel for the person accused; the Judge-Advocate, in courts-martial, shall do justice to the cause of the prisoner, by giving full weight to every circumstance or argument in his favor; shall bring the same fairly and completely into the view of the court; shall suggest the supplying of all omissions in the leading of exculpatory evidence; shall engross in the written proceedings all matters, either directly or by presumption, tending to the prisoner's defence; and finally, shall not avail himself of any advantage which superior knowledge, or ability, or his influence with the court may give him, in enforcing the conviction, rather than the acquittal of the person accused.

Many of the official functions of the Judge-Advocate, in the trial before a general court-martial, and in the matters preparatory and relative thereto, have been occasionally mentioned in the preceding chapters; but for sake of greater perspicuity, they shall be here recapitulated in a regular detail, in which may likewise be noticed such other particulars of the duty of this officer, as have not hitherto occurred to observation.

When a court-martial is summoned by the proper authority, for the trial of any military offender, the Judge-Advocate being required to attend his duty, and furnished with articles of accusation or charge, on which he is to prosecute, must, from the information of the accuser, instruct himself in all the circumstances of the case, and by what evidence the whole particulars are to be proved against the prisoners. Of these, it is proper that he should prepare, in writing, a short analysis, or plan, for his own regulation in the conduct of the trial, and examination of the witnesses. He ought then to give the earliest information to the prisoner, of the time and place appointed for his trial, and furnish him, at the same time, with a true copy of the charges that are to be exhibited against him, with the names and designations of the witnesses by which they are to be proved or supported; and likewise a correct detail of the members of the court-martial. He should, at the same time, require from the prisoner, a list of those witnesses, whom he intends to adduce in his exculpation, that the privilege may be mutual to both parties, of objecting to such evidence as they judge either inad-

CHAP. IX.

missible or of suspected credibility. The Judge-Advocate ought then to summon the witnesses for the prosecution to give their attendance at the time and place appointed; and this either by a direct intimation from himself to each of those witnesses, or by an application to the commanding officers of the regiments or corps to which they belong, requesting that they may be warned to attend that duty.

It is proper, likewise, that he should desire the prisoner to make a similar application, to enforce the attendance of the witnesses necessary for his defence. These measures ought to be taken as early as possible, that there may be sufficient time for the arrival of witnesses who may be at a distance.

It seems in no case to be improper, and may often tend to the furtherance of justice, as well as the shortning of judicial proceedings, that the Judge-Advocate, on whom lies the conduct of the evidence for the prosecution, and the discretionary power of examining such witnesses only as he may deem

CHAP. IX.

necessary, should previously be acquainted with the general nature and scope of the prisoner's defence; and for that purpose, that he should either converse with himself, or with his counsel before proceeding to trial. It has sometimes happened, that by a timely explanation in such previous conference, circumstances of the charge, apparently the most unfavorable, have been alleviated or done away, and even the necessity of a trial altogether superseded, by the anticipation which such a conference afforded, of a judgment of acquittal from the chief matters of accusation.

His duty as recorder of the court.

When the court is met for trial, and the members are regularly sworn, the Judge-Advocate, after opening the prosecution, by a recital of the charges, together with such detail of circumstances, (if the case be circumstantial and complicated) as he may deem necessary, proceeds to examine his witnesses in support of the charges; while at the same time he acts as the recorder, or clerk of the court, in taking down the evidence in writing at full length, and as nearly as possible in the words of the witnesses.

At the close of the business of each day, and in the interval, before the next meeting of the court, it is the duty of the Judge-Advocate to make a fair copy of the proceedings; which he continues thus regularly to engross, till the conclusion of the trial, when the whole is read over by him to the court, before the members proceed to deliberate and form their opinions.

Of his duty in collecting the opinions and votes of the members upon the several articles of the charge, after they have fully deliberated on the same, and lastly, in recording the final sentence of the court, we have fully treated in the preceding chapter.

The sentence of the court must be fairly engrossed, and subjoined to the record-copy of the proceedings; and the whole must be anthenticated by the signature of the President of the court, and that of the Judge-Advocate.

CHAP. IX.

It is required by the Articles of War,* that "every Judge-Advocate, or person officiating as such, at any general court-martial, shall transmit, with as much expedition as the opportunity of time and distance of place can admit, the original proceedings and sentence of such court-martial, to the Secretary of War, which said original proceedings, and sentence, shall be carefully kept and preserved in the office of the said Secretary, to the end, that the persons entitled thereto, may be enabled, upon application to the said office, to obtain copies thereof."

It is proper that the Judge-Advocate, or person officiating as such, should retain in his own possession, and carefully preserve the original minutes of the proceedings drawn up by him in court during the course of the trial, and likewise his notes of the opinions, and votes of the members; that in case of any after-questions that may be moved in the ordinary courts of law,

* Article of War 90.

CHAP. IX.

touching the conduct or result of the trial, the Judge-Advocate may have recourse to them as necessary documents, if he should be called upon to give evidence in relation thereto.

APPENDIX.

APPENDIX.

No. 1.

Form of an Order for holding a General Court-Martial.

GENERAL ORDERS.

HEAD QUARTERS,
Fort Adams, June — 1803.

A general court-martial to consist of thirteen members, will convene at Frederick-town, in the State of Maryland, on the —— day of —— for the trial of Lieutenant ——— of the Regiment of

——— and such prisoners as may be brought before it.

Colonel BURBECK, *of the Artillery, President.*

Lieut. Col. Freeman,	Members.	*Lieut. Col. Kingsbury,*
Major M'Rea,		*Major Bruff,*
Captain Freeman,		*Captain Read,*
Captain Boote,		*Captain Beal,*
Captain Saunders,		*Captain M'Clallen,*
Capt. Armistead,		*Lieutenant Osborne.*

Lieut. HOUSE, *Judge-Advocate.*

By command of the General.

T. H. CUSHING, *Adjutant and Inspector of the Army.*

No. 2.

Form of an Order for holding a General Court-Martial, when the President of the Court is only named.

GENERAL ORDERS.

HEAD QUARTERS,
Washington, July, — 1807.

A general court-martial, to consist of seven members, will convene at Fort

Jay, in the harbor of New-York, for the trial of such prisoners as may be brought before it. Lieutenant Colonel J. W. is hereby appointed President of the court-martial, and Lieutenant A. M. Judge-Advocate. The other members to be detailed by the Adjutant and Inspector of the Army.

JA. WILKINSON.

No. 3.

Form of an Order for holding a Regimental or Garrison Court-Martial.

REGIMENTAL (or GARRISON, as the case may be) ORDERS.

Fort Washington, April, — 1797.

A Regimental (or Garrison) court-martial, will assemble this day, at the orderly room, at ten o'clock, A. M.

for the trial of such prisoners as may be brought before it.

Capt. A. M. *President.*
Lieuts. A. B. & B. C. *Members.*
J. F. *Lieut. Colonel Commandant.*

No. 4.

Form of a Warrant for the holding of a Court of Inquiry, when issued from the War Office, by order of the President of the U. S. and when the Court is authorised to give its opinion on the merits of the case.

Whereas certain charges of misconduct having been alleged against Major L. M. of the —— Regiment of —— in the action of the 24th of August, 1797; a court of inquiry to consist of Lieutenant Colonel Commandant J. W. of the Artillery, President; Major R. M.

of the 1st, and Major P. G. of the 2nd Regiment of Infantry, members; is hereby appointed to examine and inquire into the nature of the aforesaid charges, which charges, together with the testimony in support thereof, will be laid before the court, by the Judge-Advocate; and the court is hereby empowered and required to give its opinion as to the real merits of the case, for the information of the President of the United States, and for so doing, this shall be a sufficient warrant.

(L.S.) Given *under my hand and seal at the War-Office of the United States, this 24th day of Sept. 1794, and of the Independence of the said States the* ——.

By command of the President of the United States of America.

H. KNOX,
Secretary of War.

No. 5.

GARRISON ORDERS.

WEST-POINT, New-York,
August 22, 1804.

In consequence of certain reports injurious to the honor and reputation of Lieutenant W. A. of the Corps of Engineers, having been circulated thro' the garrison and neighbourhood, by some person or persons unknown, a Court of Inquiry to consist of three members, is hereby appointed at the particular request of Lieutenant A. to examine and inquire into the nature of said reports, and the causes which have given rise to them.

Capt. A. M. *President.*
Lieuts. L. M. & P. Q. *Members.*
Lieut. P. W. *will act as Recorder.*

JONA. WILLIAMS;
Lieut. Col. Comdt. of the
Corps of Engineers.

No. 6.

Manner of Setting at a Court-Martial.

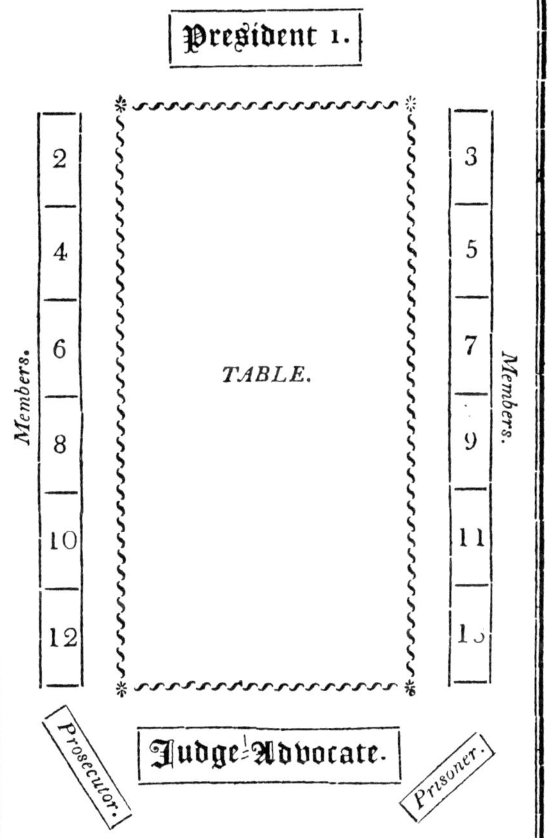

No. 7.

Form of Recording the proceedings of a Court-Martial.

Proceedings of a general court-martial, held at Fort Jay, in the harbor of New-York, by virtue of the following order:

GENERAL ORDERS.

ADJUTANT GENERAL'S OFFICE,
New-York, August 1, 1800.

A general court-martial, to consist of seven members, will assemble at Fort Jay, in the harbor of New-York, on Monday the 10th instant, at ten o'clock A. M. for the trial of such prisoners as may be brought before it.

President, Lieut. Col. W. S. SMITH, of the 12*th Regiment.*

	Members	
Maj. Hoops, of the Artil.		*Maj. Shute, of* 11*th Reg.*
Capt. Edings, of ditto.		*Capt. Huger, of the Art.*
Lieut. Walback, of Drag.		*Lt. Livingston, of* 12*reg.*

Lieut. ROBT. HEATON,
Judge-Advocate.

(Signed) WM. NORTH,
Adjutant-General.

August 10, 1800.

The court met pursuant to the above order.

PRESENT.

Lieutenant Colonel SMITH, *President.*

Major Hoops,	*Members.*	*Major Shute,*
Capt. Edings,		*Captain Huger,*
Lieut. Walback,		*Lieutenant Livingston.*

Lieut. R. HEATON,
Judge-Advocate.

The court being duly sworn in the presence of the prisoner, (or prisoners, as the case may be) proceeded to the trial of Sergeant A. B. of Capt. ——'s Company of the Regiment of —— who being previously asked if he had any objections to the members named in the general order, and replying in the negative, was arraigned on the following charge, preferred against him by Lieutenant B. C. of the Artillery.

CHARGE.

Embezzling of the public money, to the amount of 100 dollars, which sum was placed in Sergeant A. B's hands, for the purpose of recruiting, by me.

(Signed) B. C. *Lieut. of Artillery.*

To which the prisoner pleaded "not guilty."

A. A. Ensign in the 2d Regiment of Infantry, a witness for the prosecution, being duly sworn, says: On the 22d of last month, Sergeant A. B. the prisoner, was ordered by Lieut. Col. H. to proceed to Brunswick, in the State of New-Jersey, on the recruiting service, &c.

Question by the court. Did — ?
Answer. I saw Sergeant A. B. .
Question by the court — — ?
Answer — — — — — .
Question by the prisoner — — ?
Answer — — — — — .

The court adjourned to meet to-morrow morning at ten o'clock.

August 11*th*, 1800.

The court met pursuant to adjournment.

PRESENT.

Lieutenant Colonel SMITH, *President.*

Major Hoops,		*Major Shute,*
Captain Edings,	*Members.*	*Captain Huger,*
Lieut. Walback,		————

Lieut. HEATON,
Judge-Advocate.

Lieutenant Livingston being sick, and unable to attend, the court adjourned, to meet again on Thursday the 13th, at half past 9 A.M.

August the 13*th*, 1800.

The court met pursuant to adjournment.

PRESENT.

Lieutenant Colonel SMITH, *President.*

Major Hoops,		*Major Shute,*
Captain Edings,	*Members.*	*Captain Huger,*
Lieutenant Walback,		*Lieutenant Livingston.*

Lieut. HEATON,
Judge-Advocate.

Lieutenant M. P. of the 2nd Regiment of Infantry, a witness for the prosecution, being duly sworn, says: He met Sergeant A. B. the prisoner, at Brunswick, &c. &c. —— —— —— —— —— ——

Question by the court — — ?
Answer — — — — — .
Question by the prisoner — — ?
Answer — — — — — .

The evidence on the part of the prosecution being closed, Sergeant R. S. of the — Regiment of Infantry, a witness for the prisoner, being duly sworn, says: Sergeant A. B. was on the recruiting service, &c. —— —— —— —— —— ——

Question by the prisoner — — ?
Answer — — — — — .
Question by the prisoner — — ?
Answer — — — — — .
Question by the court — — ?
Answer — — — — — .

The testimony on the part of the prisoner having been heard, the prisoner requested the indulgence of the court of one day, to prepare his final defence, which was accordingly granted.

The court adjourned to meet again on the 15th inst. at 9 A.M.

August 15, 1800.

The court met pursuant to adjournment.

PRESENT.

Lieutenant Colonel SMITH, *President.*

Major Hoops, *Captain Edings,* *Lieutenant Walback,*	*Members.*	*Major Shute,* *Captain Huger,* *Lieutenant Livingston.*

Lieut. HEATON,
Judge-Advocate.

The prisoner being asked if he were ready to proceed, made the following

DEFENCE.

Mr President, and
Gentlemen of the court,

— — — — — — — —
— — — — — — — — —
— — — — — — — — —

A. B. *Sergeant.*

The court being ordered to be cleared, and the whole of the proceedings read over to the court by the Judge-Advocate, the following sentence was pronounced:

SETENCE.

The court, after mature deliberation on the testimony adduced, find the prisoner, Sergeant A. B. guilty of the charge exhibited against him, and sentence him to be reduced to the station of a private sentinel, and to undergo such monthly stoppages of half his pay, as will reimburse the United States $100, the money embezzled by him.

The court adjourned *sine die.*

WM. S. SMITH,
Lieutenant Col. Com.
12*th Reg. President.*

ROB. HEATON,
Judge-Advocate.

Usual manner of approving the Proceedings of a Court-Martial.

GENERAL ORDERS.

HEAD QUARTERS,
New-York, August 30, 1800.

At the general court-martial, of which Lieutenant Colonel Smith of the 12th Regiment is President, was tried A. B. Sergeant of Captain ——'s company of the —— Regiment of —— on the charge of "Embezzling the public money to the amount of 100 dollars, which sum was deposited in Sergeant A. B's hands, for the purpose of recruiting, by Lieutenant B. C. of the Artillery. To which charge the prisoner pleaded *Not Guilty*.

"The court, after mature deliberation, found the prisoner, Sergeant A. B. *guilty* of the charge exhibited against him; and sentenced him to be reduced to the station of a private sentinel, and to undergo such monthly stoppages of half his pay, as will reimburse the United States one hundred dollars, the money embezzled by him."

Major General Hamilton approves the sentence of the General Court-Martial, and orders the sentence to be carried into effect.

The General Court-Martial of which Colonel Smith is President, is hereby dissolved.

By command of the Major General.

Wm. NORTH, *Adjutant General.*

Articles of War.

AN ACT

For Establishing Rules and Articles for the Government of the Armies of the United States.

SECT. 1. *BE it enacted by the Senate and House of Representatives of the United States of America, in Congress assembled,* That from and after the passing of this act, the following shall be the Rules and Articles by which the Armies of the United States shall be governed:

ARTICLE I.

Every officer now in the army of the United States, shall, in six months from the passing of this act, and every Subscribing.

officer who shall hereafter be appointed, shall, before he enters on the duties of his office, subscribe these rules and regulations.

ARTICLE II.

Divine service.

It is earnestly recommended to all officers and soldiers diligently to attend divine service; and all officers who shall behave indecently or irreverently at any place of divine worship, shall, if a commissioned officer, be brought before a general court-martial, there to be publicly and severely reprimanded by the president; if non-commissioned officers or soldiers, every person so offending, shall, for his first offence, forfeit *one sixth of a dollar*, to be deducted out of his next pay; for the second offence, he shall not only forfeit a like sum, but be confined twenty-four hours; and for every like offence shall suffer and pay in like manner; which money, so forfeited, shall be applied by the captain or senior officer of the troop or company, to the use of the sick soldiers of the company or troop to which the offender belongs.

ARTICLE III.

Swearing.

Any non-commissioned officer or soldier, who shall use any profane oath or execration, shall incur the penalties expressed in the foregoing article, and a commissioned officer shall forfeit and pay for each and every such offence, one dollar, to be applied as in the preceding article.

ARTICLE IV.

Chaplain.

Ever chaplain commissioned in the army or armies of the United States, who shall absent himself from the duties assigned him (except in cases of sickness or leave of absence) shall, on conviction thereof, before a court-martial, be fined not exceeding one month's pay, besides the loss of his pay during his absence; or be discharged, as the said court-martial shall judge proper.

ARTICLE V.

Contempt of the President.

Any officer or soldier who shall use contemptuous or disrespectful words against the President of the United States, against the Vice-President thereof, against the Congress of the United States, or against the Chief Magistrate, or Legislature of any of the United States in which he may be quartered, if a commissioned officer, shall be cashiered, or otherwise punished as a court-martial shall direct; if a non-commissioned officer or soldier, he shall suffer such punishment as shall be inflicted on him by the sentence of a court-martial.

ARTICLE VI.

Contempt of the commanding officer.

Any officer or soldier who shall behave himself with contempt or disrespect towards his commanding officer, shall be punished according to the nature of his offence, by the judgment of a court-martial.

ARTICLE VII.

Mutiny, &c,

Any officer or soldier who shall begin, excite, cause or join in any mutiny or sedition in any troop or company in the service of the United States, or in any party, post, detachment or guard, shall suffer death, or such other punishment as by a court-martial shall be inflicted.

ARTICLE VIII.

Suppression of the above.

Any officer, non-commissioned officer, or soldier, who, being present at any mutiny or sedition, does not use his utmost endeavor to suppress the same, or coming to the knowledge of any intended mutiny, does not, without delay, give information thereof to his commanding officer, shall be punished by the sentence of a court-martial, with death or otherwise, according to the nature of his offence.

ARTICLE IX.

Striking superiors.

Any officer or soldier who shall strike his superior officer, or draw or lift up any weapon, or offer any violence against him, being in the execution of his office, on any pretence whatsoever, or shall disobey any lawful command of his superior officer, shall suffer death, or such other punishment as shall, according to the nature of his offence, be inflicted upon him by the sentence of a court-martial.

ARTICLE X.

Enlistment.

Every non-commissioned officer or soldier, who shall enlist himself in the service of the United States, shall, at the time of his so enlisting, or within six days afterwards, have the articles for the government of the armies of the United States, read to him, and shall, by the officer who enlisted him, or by the commanding officer of the troop or company into which he was enlisted, be taken before the next justice of the peace, or chief magistrate of any city or town corporate, not being an officer, of the army, or where recourse cannot be had to the civil magistrate, before the Judge-Advocate, and, in his presence, shall take the following oath or affirmation: "I, A. B. do solemnly swear, "or affirm, (as the case may be) that I "will bear true allegiance to the United "States of America, and that I will serve "them honestly and faithfully against all "their enemies, or opposers, whatsoever, "and observe and obey the orders of the "President of the United States, and the "orders of the officers appointed over "me, according to the rules and articles "for the government of the armies of the "United States." Which justice, magistrate, or Judge-Advocate, is to give the officer a certificate, signifying that the man enlisted, did take the said oath or affirmation. Oath of allegiance.

ARTICLE XI.

After a non-commissioned officer or soldier, shall have been duly enlisted Discharges.

and sworn, he shall not be dismissed the service without a discharge in writing; and no discharge granted to him shall be sufficient, which is not signed by a field-officer of the regiment to which he belongs, or commanding officer, where no field-officer of the regiment is present; and no discharge shall be given to a non-commissioned officer or soldier, before his term of service has expired, but by order of the President, the Secretary of War, the commanding officer of a department, or the sentence of a general court-martial, nor shall a commissioned officer be discharged the service, but by order of the President of the United States, or by sentence of a general court-martial.

ARTICLE XII.

Furloughs. Every colonel, or other officer commanding a regiment, troop, or company, and actually quartered with it, may give furloughs to non-commissioned officers or soldiers, in such numbers, and for so long a time as he shall judge to be most consistent with the good of the service; and a captain or other inferior officer commanding a troop or company, or in any garrison, fort or barrack of the United States, (his field officer being absent) may give furloughs to non-commissioned officers or soldiers, for a time not exceeding twenty days in six months, but not to more than two persons to be absent at the same time, excepting some extraordinary occasion should require it.

ARTICLE XIII.

At every muster, the commanding officer of each regiment, troop, or company there present, shall give to the commissary of musters, or other officer who musters the said regiment, troop, or company, certificates signed by himself, signifying how long such officers, as shall not appear at the said muster, have been absent, and the reason of their absence. In like manner, the commanding officer of every troop or company, shall give certificates, signifying the reasons of the absence of the non- Return Muster Rolls.

commissioned officers and private soldiers, which reasons, and time of absence, shall be inserted in the muster-rolls opposite the name of the respective absent officers and soldiers. The certificates shall, together with the muster-rolls, be remitted by the commissary of musters, or other officer mustering, to the department of war as speedily as the distance of the place will admit.

ARTICLE XIV.

False certificates.

Every officer who shall be convicted before a general court-martial, of having signed a false certificate, relating to the absence of either officer or private soldier, or relative to his or their pay, shall be cashiered.

ARTICLE XV.

False musters.

Every officer who shall knowingly make a false muster of man or horse, and every officer or commissary of musters, who shall willingly sign, direct or allow the signing of muster-rolls, wherein such false muster is contained, shall, upon proof made thereof by two witnesses, before a general court-martial, be cashiered, and shall be thereby utterly disabled to have or hold any office or employment in the service of the United States.

ARTICLE XVI.

Commissary.

Any commissary of musters or other officer, who shall be convicted of having taken money or other thing by way of gratification, on mustering any regiment, troop, or company, or on the signing muster-rolls, shall be displaced from his office, and shall be thereby, utterly disabled to have or hold any office or employment in the service of the United States.

ARTICLE XVII.

Musters.

Any officer who shall presume to muster a person as a soldier, who is not a soldier, shall be deemed guilty of having made a false muster, and shall suffer accordingly.

ARTICLE XVIII.

False returns.

Every officer who shall knowingly make a false return to the department of war, or to any of his superior officers authorised to call for such returns of the state of the regiment, troop or company, or garrison, under his command; or of the arms, ammunition, clothing, or other stores thereunto belonging, shall, on conviction thereof before a court-martial, be cashiered.

ARTICLE XIX.

Monthly returns.

The commanding officer of every regiment, troop, or independent company, or garrison of the United States, shall, in the beginning of every month, remit, through the proper channels, to the department of war, an exact return of the regiment, troop, independent company, or garrison under his command, specifying the names of officers then absent from their posts, with the reasons for, and the time of their absence. And any officer who shall be convicted of having, through neglect, or design, omitted sending such returns, shall be punished according to the nature of his crime, by the judgment of a general court-martial.

ARTICLE XX.

Desertion

All officers and soldiers, who have received pay, or have been duly enlisted in the Service of the United States, and shall be convicted of having deserted the same, shall suffer death, or such other punishment as by sentence of a court-martial shall be inflicted.

ARTICLE XXI.

Absent without leave.

Any non-commissioned officer or soldier, who shall, without leave from his commanding officer, absent himself from his troop, company, or detachment, shall, upon being convicted thereof, be punished according to the nature of his offence at the discretion of a court-martial.

ARTICLE XXII.

Penalty on enlisting deserters.

No non-commissioned officer or soldier, shall enlist himself in any other regiment, troop, or company, without a regular discharge from the regiment, troop, or company, in which he last served, on the penalty of being reputed a deserter, and suffering accordingly. And in case any officer shall knowingly receive and entertain such non-commissioned officer or soldier, or shall not, after his being discovered to be a deserter, immediately confine him, and give notice thereof to the corps in which he last served, the said officer shall by a court-martial be cashiered.

ARTICLE XXIII.

Penalty on advising desertion.

Any officer or soldier, who shall be convicted of having advised or persuaded any other officer or soldier, to desert the service of the United States, shall suffer death, or such other punishment as shall be inflicted upon him by the sentence of a court-martial.

ARTICLE XXIV.

No officer or soldier shall use any reproachful or provoking speeches or gestures to another, upon pain, if an officer, of being put in arrest; if a soldier, confined, and of asking pardon of the party offended, in the presence of his commanding officer. Provoking speeches, &c.

ARTICLE XXV.

No officer or soldier shall send a challenge to another officer or soldier, to fight a duel, or accept a challenge, if sent; upon pain, if a commissioned officer, of being cashiered: if a non-commissioned officer or soldier, of suffering corporal punishment at the discretion of a court-martial. Duelling.

ARTICLE XXVI.

If any commissioned or non-commissioned officer commanding a guard, Wilfully suffering duels, &c.

shall knowingly or willingly suffer any person whatsoever to go forth to fight a duel, he shall be punished as a challenger; and all seconds, promoters, and carriers of challenges, in order to duels, shall be deemed principals, and be punished accordingly. And it shall be the duty of every officer, commanding an army, regiment, company, post, or detachment, who is knowing to a challenge being given, or accepted, by any officer, non-commissioned officer, or soldier, under his command, or has reason to believe the same to be the case, immediately to arrest and bring to trial such offenders.

ARTICLE XXVII.

Challenging.

All officers, of what condition soever, have power to part and quell all quarrels, frays, and disorders, though the persons concerned should belong to another regiment, troop, or company; and either to order officers into arrest, or non-commissioned officers into confinement, until their proper superior officers shall be acquainted therewith: and whosoever shall refuse to obey such officer, (though of an inferior rank) or shall draw his sword upon him, shall be punished at the discretion of a general court-martial.

ARTICLE XXVIII.

Any officer or soldier, who shall upbraid another for refusing a challenge, shall himself be punished as a challenger; and all officers and soldiers are hereby discharged from any disgrace, or opinion of disadvantage, which might arise from their having refused to accept of challenges, as they will only have acted in obedience to the laws, and done their duty as good soldiers, who subject themselves to discipline. Upbraiding.

ARTICLE XXIX.

No suttler shall be permitted to sell any kind of liquors or victuals, or to keep their houses or shops open for the entertainment of soldiers, after nine at Suttlers.

night, or before the beating of the reveilles, or upon Sundays, during Divine service, or sermon, on the penalty of being dismissed from all future suttling.

ARTICLE XXX.

Suttling. All officers, commanding in the field, forts, barracks, or garrisons, of the United States, are hereby required to see that the persons permitted to suttle, shall supply the soldiers with good and wholesome provisions, or other articles, at a reasonable price, as they shall be answerable for their neglect.

ARTICLE XXXI.

Suttling. No officer commanding in any of the garrisons, forts, or barracks, of the United States, shall exact exorbitant prices for houses or stalls let out to suttlers, or connive at the like exactions in others; nor by his own authority, and for his private advantage, lay any duty or imposition upon, or be interested in the sale of any victuals, liquors, or other necessaries of life, brought into the garrison, fort, or barracks, for the use of the soldiers, on the penalty of being discharged from the service.

ARTICLE XXXII.

Justice and good order.

Every officer commanding in quarters, garrisons, or on the march, shall keep good order, and to the utmost of his power, redress all abuses or disorders, which may be committed by any officer or soldier under his command; if upon complaint made to him of officers or soldiers beating, or otherwise ill-treating any person; of disturbing fairs, or markets, or of committing any kinds of riots, to the disquieting of the citizens of the United States, he, the said commander, who shall refuse, or omit to see justice done to the offender or offenders, and reparation made to the party or parties injured, as far as part of the offenders pay shall enable him or them, shall, upon proof thereof, be cashiered, or punished as a general court-martial shall direct.

ARTICLE XXXIII.

Capital crimes.

When any commissioned officer or soldier, shall be accused of a capital crime, or of having used violence, or committed any offence against the persons or property of any citizen of any of the United States, such as is punishable by the known laws of the land, the commanding officer, and officers of every regiment, troop, or company, to which the person or persons, so accused, shall belong, are hereby required, upon application duly made by, or in behalf of the party, or parties injured, to use their utmost endeavors to deliver over such accused person or persons, to the civil magistrate, and likewise to be aiding and assisting to the officers of justice, in apprehending and securing the person or persons so accused, in order to bring him or them to trial. If any commanding officer or officers, shall wilfully neglect, or shall refuse, upon the application aforesaid, to deliver over such accused person or persons, to the civil magistrates, or to be aiding and assisting to the officers of justice in apprehending such person or persons, the officer or officers, so offending, shall be cashiered.

ARTICLE XXXIV.

Redress for officers.

If any officer shall think himself wronged by his colonel, or the commanding officer of the regiment, and shall, upon due application being made to him, be refused redress, he may complain to the general, commanding in the state, or territory, where such regiment shall be stationed, in order to obtain justice; who is hereby required to examine into the said complaint, and take proper measures for redressing the wrong complained of, and transmit as soon as possible, to the department of war, a true state of such complaint, with the proceedings had thereon.

ARTICLE XXXV.

Redress for inferior officers and soldiers.

If any inferior officer, or soldier, shall think himself wronged by his captain, or other officer, he is to complain thereof to the commanding officer of the regiment, who is hereby required to summon a regimental court-martial, for the doing justice to the complainant; from which regimental court-martial, either party may, if he thinks himself still aggrieved, appeal to a general court-martial. But if, upon a second hearing, the appeal shall appear vexatious and groundless, the person so appealing, shall be punished at the discretion of the said court-martial.

ARTICLE XXXVI.

Store-keeper and commissary.

Any commissioned officer, store-keeper, or commissary, who shall be convicted at a general court-martial, of having sold, without a proper order for that purpose, embezzled, misapplied, or wilfully, or through neglect, suffered any of the provisions, forage, arms, clothing, ammunition, or other military stores belonging to the United States, to be spoiled or damaged, shall, at his own expense, make good the loss or damage, and shall, moreover, forfeit all his pay, and be dismissed the service.

ARTICLE XXXVII.

Punishment for selling, &c.

Any non-commissioned officer or soldier, who shall be convicted at a regimental court-martial, of having sold, or designedly, or through neglect, wasted the ammunition delivered out to him, to be employed in the service of the United States, shall be punished at the discretion of such court.

ARTICLE XXXVIII.

Penalty on losing, selling, or spoiling arms.

Every non-commissioned officer or soldier, who shall be convicted before a court-martial, of having sold, lost, or spoiled, through neglect, his horse, arms, clothes, or accoutrements, shall bc put under such weekly stoppages (not exceeding the half of his pay) as such court-martial shall judge sufficient for repairing the loss or damage; and shall suffer confinement, or such other corporeal punishment as his crime shall deserve.

ARTICLE XXXIX.

Penalty on officers embezzling, &c.

Every officer who shall be convicted before a court-martial, of having embezzled, or misplaced any money, with which he may have been entrusted for the payment of the men under his command, or for enlisting men into the service, or for other purposes, if a commissioned officer, shall be cashiered, and compelled to refund the money; if a non-commissioned officer, shall be reduced to the ranks, be put under stoppages until the money be made good, and suffer such corporeal punishment as such court-martial shall direct.

ARTICLE XL.

Captains accountable for arms, &c.

Every captain of a troop or company is charged with the arms, accoutrements, ammunition, clothing, or other warlike stores belonging to the troop, or company, under his command, which he is to be accountable for to his colonel, in case of their being lost, spoiled, or damaged, not by unavoidable accidents, or on actual service.

ARTICLE XLI.

All non-commissioned officers and soldiers, who shall be found one mile from the camp, without leave, in writing, from their commanding officer, shall suffer such punishment as shall be inflicted upon them by the sentence of a court-martial.

Non-commissioned officers & soldiers, not to go one mile from camp

ARTICLE XLII.

No officer or soldier shall lie out of his quarters, garrison, or camp, without leave from his superior officer, upon penalty of being punished according to the nature of his offence, by the sentence of a court-martial.

Officers & soldiers, not to lie out of their quarters.

ARTICLE XLIII.

Every non-commissioned officer and soldier shall retire to his quarters, or tent, at the beating of the retreat; in de-

Non-commissioned officers & soldiers to retire to

their tents at the beating the retreat.

fault of which he shall be punished according to the nature of his offence.

ARTICLE XLIV.

Absence from parade.

No officer, non-commissioned officer, or soldier, shall fail in repairing at the time fixed, to the place of parade, of exercise, or other rendezvous, appointed by his commanding officer, if not prevented by sickness, or some other evident necessity; or shall go from the said place of rendezvous, without leave from his commanding officer, before he shall be regularly dismissed or relieved, on the penalty of being punished according to the nature of his offence, by the sentence of a court-martial.

ARTICLE XLV.

Punishment for drunkenness.

Any commissioned officer who shall be found drunk on his guard, party, or other duty, shall be cashiered. Any non-commissioned officer or soldier so offending, shall suffer such corporeal punishment as shall be inflicted by the sentence of a court-martial.

ARTICLE XLVI.

Any sentinel who shall be found sleeping upon his post, or shall leave it before he shall be regularly relieved, shall suffer death, or such other punishment as shall be inflicted by the sentence of a court-martial. Sleeping on post.

ARTICLE XLVII.

No soldier belonging to any regiment, troop, or company, shall hire another to do his duty for him, or be excused from duty, but in cases of sickness, disability, or leave of absence; and every such soldier found guilty of hiring his duty, as also the party so hired to do another's duty, shall be punished at the discretion of a regimental court-martial. Hiring of duty.

ARTICLE XLVIII.

And every non-commissioned officer conniving at such hiring of duty afore- Conniving at, do.

said, shall be reduced; and every commissioned officer, knowing and allowing such ill practices in the service, shall be punished by the judgment of a general court-martial.

ARTICLE XLIX.

False alarms.

Any officer belonging to the service of the United States, who, by discharging of fire arms, drawing of swords, beating of drums, or by any other means whatsoever, shall occasion false alarms in camp, garrison, or quarters, shall suffer death, or such other punishment as shall be ordered by the sentence of a general court-martial.

ARTICLE L.

Quitting platoons.

Any officer or soldier, who shall, without urgent necessity, or without the leave of his superior officer, quit his guard, platoon, or division, shall be punished according to the nature of his offence, by the sentence of a court-martial.

ARTICLE LI.

No officer or soldier shall do violence to any person who brings provisions, or other necessaries to the camp, garrison, or quarters, of the forces of the United States, employed in any parts of the said States, upon pain of death, or such other punishment as a court-martial shall direct. Violence.

ARTICLE LII.

Any officer or soldier, who shall misbehave himself before the enemy, run away, or shamefully abandon any fort, post, or guard, which he or they may be commanded to defend, or speak words inducing others to do the like: or shall cast away his arms and ammunition, or who shall quit his post or colours to plunder and pillage, every such offender, being duly convicted thereof, shall suffer death, or such other punishment as shall be ordered by the sentence of a general court-martial. Cowardice

ARTICLE LIII.

Making known the watch-word.

Any person belonging to the armies of the United States, who shall make known the watch-word to any person who is not entitled to receive it, according to the rules and discipline of war, or shall presume to give a parole or watch-word, different from what he received, shall suffer death or such other punishment as shall be ordered by the sentence of a general court-martial.

ARTICLE LIV.

Punishment for improper destruction.

All officers and soldiers are to behave themselves orderly in quarters, and on their march; and whosoever shall commit any waste or spoil, either in walks of trees, parks, warrens, fish-ponds, houses, or gardens, corn-fields, enclosures of meadows, or shall maliciously destroy any property whatsoever, belonging to the inhabitants of the United States, unless by order of the then commander in chief of the armies of the said States, shall (besides such penalties as they are liable to by law) be punished, according to the nature and degree of the offence, by the judgment of a regimental or general court-martial.

ARTICLE LV.

Forcing a safe-guard.

Whosoever, belonging to the armies of the United States, employed in foreign parts, shall force a safe-guard, shall suffer death.

ARTICLE LVI.

Relieving an enemy.

Whosoever shall relieve the enemy with money, victuals, or ammunition, or shall knowingly harbor or protect an enemy, shall suffer death, or such other punishment as shall be ordered by the sentence of a court-martial.

ARTICLE LVII.

Corresponding with the enemy.

Whosoever shall be convicted of holding correspondence with, or giving intelligence to the enemy, either directly or indirectly, shall suffer death, or such other punishment as shall be ordered by the sentence of a court-martial.

ARTICLE LVIII.

Captured stores.

All public stores taken in the enemy's camp, towns, forts, or magazines, whether of artillery, ammunition, clothing, forage, or provisions, shall be secured for the service of the United States; for the neglect of which the commanding officer is to be answerable.

ARTICLE LIX.

Surrendering posts.

If any commander of any garrison, fortress, or post, shall be compelled by the officers and soldiers under his command, to give up to the enemy, or to abandon it, the commissioned officers, non-commissioned officers or soldiers, who shall be convicted of having so offended, shall suffer death, or such other punishment as shall be inflicted upon them by the sentence of a court-martial.

ARTICLE LX.

All suttlers and retainers to the camp, and all persons whatsoever, serving with the armies of the United States, in the field, though not enlisted soldiers, are to be subject to orders, according to the rules and discipline of war. Suttlers.

ARTICLE LXI.

Officers having brevetts, or commissions, of a prior date to those of the regiment in which they serve, may take place in courts-martial and on detachments, when composed of different corps, according to the ranks given them in their brevetts, or dates of their former commissions; but in the regiment, troop, or company, to which such officers belong, they shall do duty, and take rank, both in courts-martial and on detachments, which shall be composed only of their own corps, according to the commissions by which they are mustered in the said corps. Brevetts.

ARTICLE LXII.

Command and rank.

If upon marches, guards, or in quarters, different corps of the army shall happen to join, or do duty together, the officer highest in rank of the line of the army, marine corps, or militia, by commission there, on duty, or in quarters, shall command the whole, and give orders for what is needful to the service, unless otherwise specially directed by the President of the United States, according to the nature of the case.

ARTICLE LXIII.

Engineers.

The functions of the engineers being generally confined to the most elevated branch of military science, they are not to assume, nor are they subject to be ordered on any duty beyond the line of their immediate profession, except by the special order of the President of the United States, but they are to receive every mark of respect, to which their rank in the army may entitle them, respectively, and are liable to be transferred, at the discretion of the President, from one corps to another, regard being paid to rank.

ARTICLE LXIV.

General courts-martial. General courts-martial may consist of any number of commissioned officers, from five to thirteen inclusively; but they shall not consist of less than thirteen, where that number can be convened without manifest injury to the service.

ARTICLE LXV.

Ditto. Any general officer commanding an army, or colonel commanding a separate department, may appoint general courts-martial, whenever necessary. But no sentence of a court-martial shall be carried into execution, until after the whole proceedings shall have been laid before the officer ordering the same, or the officer commanding the troops, for the time being; neither shall any sentence of a general court-martial, in time of peace, extending to the loss of life, or the dismission of a commissioned officer, or which shall, either in time of peace or war, respecting a general officer, be carried into execution, until after the whole proceedings shall have been transmitted to the secretary of war, to be laid before the President of the United States, for his confirmation or disapproval, and orders in the case. All other sentences may be confirmed and executed by the officer ordering the court to assemble, or the commanding officer, for the time being, as the case may be.

ARTICLE LXVI.

General courts-martial.

Every officer commanding a regiment or corps, may appoint for his own regiment or corps, courts-martial, to consist of three commissioned officers, for the trial and punishment of offences, not capital, and decide upon their sentences. For the same purpose, all officers commanding any of the garrisons, forts, barracks, or other places, where the troops consist of different corps, may assemble courts-martial, to consist of three commissioned officers, and decide upon their sentences.

ARTICLE LXVII.

No garrison, or regimental court-martial, shall have the power to try capital cases, or commissioned officers; neither shall they inflict a fine exceeding one month's pay, nor imprison, nor put to hard labor, any non-commissioned officer or soldier, for a longer time than one month. General courts-martial.

ARTICLE LXVIII.

Whenever it may be found convenient and necessary to the public service, the officers of the marine shall be associated with the officers of the land forces, for the purpose of holding courts-martial and trying offenders belonging to either; and in such cases the orders of the senior officers of either corps, who may be present and duly authorised, shall be received and obeyed. Ditto.

ARTICLE LXIX.

Judge-Advocate, and oaths.

The Judge-Advocate, or some person deputed by him, or by the general, or officer commanding the army, detachment, or garrison, shall prosecute in the name of the United States, but shall so far consider himself as counsel for the prisoner, after the said prisoner shall have made his plea, as to object to any leading question to any of the witnesses, or any question to the prisoner, the answer to which might tend to criminate himself; and administer to each member of the court, before they proceed upon any trial, the following oath, which shall also be taken by all members of the regimental and garrison courts-martial:—" You A. B. do " swear, that you will well and truly " try and determine, according to evi- " dence, the matter now before you, " between the United States of Ameri- " ca, and the prisoner to be tried; and " that you will duly administer justice, " according to the provisions of ' An

" Act establishing Rules and Articles " for the Government of the Armies of " the United States,' without partiality, " favor or affection; and if any doubt " shall arise, not explained by said ar- " ticles, according to your conscience, " the best of your understanding, and " the custom of war, in like cases: and " you do further swear, that you will " not divulge the sentence of the court, " until it shall be published by the proper " authority; neither will you disclose or " discover the vote or opinion of any " particular member of the court-mar- " tial, unless required to give evidence " thereof as a witness, by a court of jus- " tice, in a due course of law.—*So help* " *you God!*"

And as soon as the said oath shall have been administered to the respective members, the president of the court shall administer to the Judge-Advocate, or person officiating as such, an oath in the following words:

" You A. B. do swear, that you will " not disclose or discover the vote or " opinion of any particular member of

" the court-martial, unless required to
" give evidence thereof, as a witness,
" by a court of justice, in due course of
" law; nor divulge the sentence of the
" court to any but the proper authority,
" until it shall be duly disclosed by the
" same.—*So help you God!*"

ARTICLE LXX.

Mute or perverse prisoners.

When a prisoner arraigned before a general court-martial, shall, from obstinate and deliberate design, stand mute, or answer foreign to the purpose, the court may proceed to trial and judgment, as if the prisoner had regularly pleaded not guilty.

ARTICLE LXXI.

Challenge.

When a member shall be challenged by a prisoner, he must state his cause of challenge, or which the court shall, after due deliberation, determine the relevancy or validity, and decide accordingly; and no challenge to more than one member, at a time, shall be received by the court.

ARTICLE LXXII.

All the members of a court-martial, are to behave with decency and calmness; and in giving their votes, are to begin with the youngest in commission. Form of voting in courts-martial.

ARTICLE LXXIII.

All persons who give evidence before a court-martial, are to be examined on oath or affirmation, in the following form: Oath of evidence.

"You swear or affirm, (as the case
"may be) the evidence you shall give,
"in the cause now in hearing, shall be
"the truth, the whole truth, and no-
"thing but the truth.—*So help you*
"*God!*"

ARTICLE LXXIV.

On the trials of cases not capital, before courts-martial, the deposition of Depositions before justices.

witnesses, not in the line or staff of the army, may be taken before some justice of the peace, and read in evidence, provided the prosecutor and the person accused, are present at the taking of the same, or are duly notified thereof.

ARTICLE LXXV.

Officers only to be tried by general courts-martial.

No officer shall be tried but by a general court-martial, nor by officers of inferior rank, if it can be avoided. Nor shall any proceedings or trials be carried on, excepting between the hours of eight in the morning and three in the afternoon, excepting in cases, which, in the opinion of the officer appointing the court-martial, require immediate example.

ARTICLE LXXVI.

Menacing words, or gestures.

No person whatsoever, shall use any menacing words, signs or gestures, in presence of a court-martial, or shall cause any disorder, or riot, or disturb their proceedings, on the penalty of being punished at the discretion of the said court-martial.

ARTICLE LXXVII.

Whenever any officer shall be charged with a crime, he shall be arrested, and confined in his barracks, quarters, or tents, and deprived of his sword by the commanding officer. And any officer, who shall leave his confinement before he shall be set at liberty, by his commanding officer, or by a superior officer, shall be cashiered. Arrest of officers.

ARTICLE LXXVIII.

Non-commissioned officers and soldiers, charged with crimes, shall be confined, until they shall be tried by a court-martial, or released by proper authority. Non-commissioned officers & soldiers accused.

ARTICLE LXXIX.

No officer or soldier, who shall be put in arrest shall continue in confine- Term of confinement.

ment more than eight days, or until such time as a court-martial can be assembled.

ARTICLE LXXX.

Officers to receive prisoners.

No officer commanding a guard or provost-martial, shall refuse to receive or keep any prisoner committed to his charge by any officer belonging to the forces of the United States: provided the officer committing, shall at the same time, deliver an account in writing, signed by himself, of the crime with which the said prisoner is charged.

ARTICLE LXXXI.

Officers not to release prisoners.

No officer commanding a guard or provost-martial, shall presume to release any person committed to his charge, without proper authority for so doing; nor shall he suffer any person to escape, on the penalty of being punished for it, by the sentence of a court-martial.

ARTICLE LXXXII.

Every officer or provost-martial, to whose charge prisoners shall be committed, shall, within twenty four hours after such commitment, or as soon as he shall be relieved from his guard, make report, in writing, to the commanding officer, of their names, their crimes, and the names of the officers who committed them, on the penalty of being punished for disobedience or neglect, at the discretion of a court-martial. Officers to report prisoners.

ARTICLE LXXXIII.

Any commissioned officer, convicted before a general court-martial, of conduct unbecoming an officer and a gentleman, shall be dismissed the service. Unbecoming conduct in officers.

ARTICLE LXXXIV.

In cases, where a court-martial may think it proper to sentence a commis- Sentence of courts-martial.

sioned officer to be suspended from command, they shall have power also to suspend his pay and emoluments from the same time, according to the nature and heinousness of the offence.

ARTICLE LXXXV.

Cowardice or fraud, to be published.

In all cases, where a commissioned officer is cashiered for cowardice or fraud, it shall be added in the sentence, that the crime, name, and place of abode, and punishment of the delinquent, be published in the news-papers, in and about the camp, and of the particular state from which the offender came, or where he usually resides; after which it shall be deemed scandalous for an officer to associate with him.

ARTICLE LXXXVI.

Transportation of accused persons.

The commanding officer of any post or detachment, in which there shall not be a number of officers adequate to form a general court-martial, shall, in cases which require the cognizance of such a court, report to the commanding officer of the department, who shall order a court to be assembled at the nearest post or detachment, and the party accused, with the necessary witnesses, to be transported to the place where the said court shall be assembled.

ARTICLE LXXXVII.

Death and whipping.

No person shall be sentenced to suffer death, but by the concurrence of two thirds of the members of a general court-martial, nor, except in the cases herein expressly mentioned; nor shall more than fifty lashes be inflicted on any offender, at the discretion of a court-martial; and no officer, non-commissioned officer, soldier, or follower of the army, shall be tried a second time for the same offence.

ARTICLE LXXXVIII.

Limitation

No person shall be liable to be tried and punished by a general court-martial for any offence, which shall appear to have been committed more than two years before the issuing of the order for such trial, unless the person, by reason of having absented himself, or some other manifest impediment shall not have been amenable to justice within that period.

ARTICLE LXXXIX.

Powers of officers authorising courts-martial.

Every officer authorised to order a general court-martial, shall have power to pardon or mitigate any punishment ordered by such court, except the sentence of death, or of cashiering an officer; which, in the cases where he has authority (by Article 65) to carry them into execution, he may suspend until the pleasure of the President of the United States can be known; which suspension, together with copies of the proceedings of the court-martial, the said officer shall immediately transmit to the President for his determination. And the colonel or commanding officer of the regiment or garrison, where any regimental or garrison court-martial shall be held, may pardon or mitigate any punishment ordered by such court to be inflicted.

ARTICLE XC.

Judge-Advocate, and rights of accused.

Every Judge-Advocate, or person officiating as such, at any general court-martial, shall transmit, with as much expedition as the opportunity of time and distance of place can admit, the original proceedings and sentence of such court-martial, to the secretary of war, which said original proceedings and sentence shall be carefully kept and preserved in the office of the said secretary, to the end that the persons entitled thereto may be enabled, upon application to the said office, to obtain copies thereof.

The party tried by any general court-martial, shall, upon demand thereof made by himself, or by any person or persons in his behalf, be entitled to a copy of the sentence and proceedings of such court-martial.

ARTICLE XCI.

Courts of inquiry.

In cases where the general, or commanding officer may order a court of inquiry, to examine into the nature of any transaction, accusation or imputation against any officer or soldier, the said court shall consist of one or more officers, not exceeding three, and a Judge-Advocate, or other suitable person, as a recorder, to reduce the proceedings and evidence to writing, all of whom shall be sworn to the faithful performance of their duty. This court shall have the same power to summon witnesses as a court-martial, and to examine them on oath. But they shall not give their opinion on the merits of the case, excepting they shall be thereto specially required. The parties accused shall also be permitted to cross-examine and interrogate the witnesses, so as to investigate fully the circumstances in question.

ARTICLE XCII.

The proceedings of a court of inquiry must be authenticated by the signature of the recorder, and the president, and delivered to the commanding officer; and the said proceedings may be admitted as evidence, by a court-martial, in cases not capital, or extending to the dismission of an officer: provided that the circumstances are such, that oral testimony cannot be obtained. But as courts of inquiry may be perverted to dishonorable purposes, and may be considered as engines of destruction to military merit, in the hands of weak, and envious commandants, they are hereby prohibited, unless directed by the President of the United States, or demanded by the accused. Courts of inquiry to be authenticated.

ARTICLE XCIII.

The Judge-Advocate, or recorder, shall administer to the members the following oath: Judge-Advocate, and witnesses' oath.

"You shall well and truly examine "and inquire, according to your evi- "dence, into the matter now before you, "without partiality, favor, affection, "prejudice, or hope of reward.—*So* "*help you God!*"

After which, the president shall administer to the Judge-Advocate or recorder, the following oath:

"You A. B. do swear, that you will, "according to your best abilities, accu- "rately and impartially, record the pro- "ceedings of the court, and the evi- "dence to be given in the case in hear- "ing.—*So help you God!*"

The witnesses shall take the same oath as witnesses sworn before a court-martial.

ARTICLE XCIV.

Commissioned officers who may die.

When any commissioned officer shall die, or be killed in the service of the United States, the major of the regiment, or the officer doing the major's duty in his absence, or in any post or garrison, the second officer in command, or the assistant military agent, shall immediately secure all his effects or equipage then in camp or quarters, and shall make an inventory thereof, and forthwith transmit the same to the office of the department of war, to the end, that his executors or administrators may receive the same.

ARTICLE XCV.

Non-commissioned officers and soldiers, who may die or be killed.

When any non-commissioned officer or soldier shall die, or be killed in the service of the United States, the then commanding officer of the troop, or company, shall, in the presence of two other commissioned officers, take an account of what effects he died possessed of, above his arms and accoutrements, and transmit the same to the office of the department of war; which said effects are to be accounted for, and paid to the representatives of such deceased non-commissioned officer or soldier. And in case any of the officers, so authorised to take care of the effects of deceased officers and soldiers, should, before they have accounted to their representatives for the same, have occasion to leave the regiment, or post, by preferment, or otherwise, they shall, before they be permitted to quit the same, deposit in the hands of the commanding officer, or of the assistant military agent, all the effects of such deceased non-commissioned officers and soldiers, in order that the same may be secured for, and paid to their respective representatives.

ARTICLE XCVI.

Officers, &c. in the artillery to be subject to be tried by courts-martial.

All officers, conductors, gunners, matrosses, drivers, or other persons whatsoever, receiving pay, or hire, in the service of the artillery or corps of engineers of the United States, shall be governed by the aforesaid rules and articles, and shall be subject to be tried by courts-martial, in like manner with the officers and soldiers of the other troops in the service of the United States.

ARTICLE XCVII.

Officers, &c. of militia, &c. mustered and in the pay of the United States, to be governed by the rules and articles of war, and subject to courts-martial.

The officers and soldiers of any troops, whether militia or others, being mustered and in pay of the United States, shall, at all times, and in all places, when joined, or acting in conjunction with the regular forces of the United States, be governed by these rules and articles of war, and shall be subject to be tried by courts-martial, in like manner with the officers and soldiers in the regular forces, save only, that such courts-martial shall be composed entirely of militia officers.

ARTICLE XCVIII.

Officers serving under the authority of states.

All officers, serving by commission from the authority of any particular state, shall, on all detachments, courts-martial, or other duty, wherein they may be employed in conjunction with the regular forces of the United States, take rank, next after all officers of the like grade in said regular forces, notwithstanding the commissions of such militia or state officers may be elder than the commissions of the officers of the regular forces of the United States.

ARTICLE XCIX.

Crimes not capital cognizable by general, or regimental courts-martial.

All crimes not capital, and all disorders and neglects which officers and soldiers may be guilty of, to the prejudice of good order and military discipline, though not mentioned in the foregoing articles of war, are to be taken cognizance of by a general or regimental court-martial, according to the nature and degree of the offence, and be punished at their discretion.

ARTICLE C.

President of the U. States to prescribe the uniform.

The President of the United States, shall have power to prescribe the uniform of the army.

ARTICLE CI.

Articles to be read & published every six months.

The foregoing articles are to be read and published once every six months, to every garrison, regiment, troop or company, mustered, or to be mustered in the service of the United States, and are to be duly observed and obeyed, by all officers and soldiers, who are, or shall be in said service.

Spies to suffer death.

SECT. 2. *And be it further enacted*, That in time of war, all persons not citizens of, or owing allegiance to the United States of America, who shall be found lurking as spies, in, or about the fortifications, or encampments of the armies of the United States, or any of them, shall suffer death, according to the law and usuge of nations, by sentence of a general court-martial.

Preceding rules and regulations abolished.

SECT. 3. *And be it further enacted*, That the rules and regulations by which the armies of the United States have heretofore been governed, and the resolves of Congress thereunto annexed, and respecting the same, shall henceforth be void and of no effect, except so far as may relate to any transactions under them, prior to the promulgation of this act, at the several posts and garrisons respectively, occupied by any part of the army of the United States.

NATHL. MACON,
Speaker of the House of Representatives.

S. SMITH,
President of the Senate, pro tempore.

April 10, 1806.

APPROVED,

TH: JEFFERSON.

EXTRACT

From an Act fixing the Military Establishment of the United States.

SECT. 10. *And be it further enacted*, That the officers, non-commissioned officers, musicians and privates of the said corps, shall be governed by the rules and articles of war, which have been established by the United States in congress assembled, or by such rules and articles as may be hereafter, by law, established: *Provided nevertheless*, That the sentence of general courts-martial, extending to the loss of life, the dismission of a commissioned officer, or which shall respect the general officer, shall, with the whole of the proceedings of such cases, respectively, be laid before the President of the United States, who is hereby authorised to direct the same

The troops to be governed by the articles and rules of war, now in force; and such others as may be made;—sentences of general courts-martial, with their proceedings, be laid before the President, in certain cases.

to be carried into execution, or otherwise, as he shall judge proper.

Additional penalty to non-commissioned officers, &c. for desertion;

Sect. 18. *And be it further enacted*, That if any non-commissioned officer, musician or private, shall desert the service of the United States, he shall, in addition to the penalties mentioned in the rules and articles of war, be liable to serve, for and during such a period, as shall, with the time he may have served previous to his desertion, amount to the full term of his enlistment; and such soldier shall and may be tried by a court-martial, and punished, although the term of his enlistment may have elapsed previous to his being apprehended or tried.

they may be tried & punished, if apprehended after the term for which enlisted.

Sect. 19. *And be it further enacted*, That every person who shall procure or entice a soldier in the service of the United States to desert, or who shall purchase from any soldier his arms, uniform clothing, or any part thereof; and every captain or commanding officer of any ship or vessel, who shall enter on board such ship or vessel, as one of his crew, knowing him to have de-

Persons concerned in procuring, or assisting, in the desertion of soldiers, or who shall purchase their uniform clothing, may be fined or imprisoned at the discretion serted, or otherwise carry away any such soldier, or shall refuse to deliver him up to the orders of his commanding officer, shall, upon legal conviction, be fined at the discretion of any court having cognizance of the same, in any sum not exceeding three hundred dollars, or be imprisoned any term not exceeding one year. of certain courts.

SECT. 20. *And be it further enacted*, That every officer, non-commissioned officer, musician and private, shall take and subscribe the following oath or affirmation, to wit:

"I, A. B. do solemnly swear or affirm, (as the case may be) that I will bear true faith and allegiance to the United States of America, and that I will serve them honestly and faithfully against their enemies or opposers, whomsoever; and that I will observe and obey the orders of the President of the United States, and the orders of the officers appointed over me, according to the rules and articles of war." Oath to be taken by officers, musicians, and privates.

In case of a general court-martial the President may appoint a Judge-Advocate;

An additional allowance to the Judge-Advocate;

Brigadier general to appoint in cases that the President does not.

SECT. 21. *And be it further enacted*, That whenever a general court-martial shall be ordered, the President of the United States may appoint some fit person to act as Judge-Advocate, who shall be allowed, in addition to his other pay, one dollar and twenty-five cents for every day he shall be necessarily employed in the duties of the said court; and in cases where the President shall not have made such appointment, the brigadier-general or the president of the court may make the same.

Provision to commissioned officers for extra expenses, in travelling to and sitting on general courts-martial.

SECT. 22. *And be it further enacted*, That where any commissioned officer shall be obliged to incur any extra expense in travelling and sitting on general courts-martial, he shall be allowed a reasonable compensation for such extra expense actually incurred, not exceeding one dollar and twenty-five cents per day, to officers who are not entitled to forage, and not exceeding one dollar per day to such as shall be entitled to forage.

Non-commissioned officers &

SECT. 23. *And be it further enacted*, That no non-commissioned officer, musician or private shall be arrested, or subject to arrest, or to be taken in execution for any debt under the sum of twenty dollars, contracted before enlistment, nor for any debt contracted after enlistment.

privates to be free from arrest for debts under 20 dollars contracted before enlistment, and for all while in service.

THE CONSTITUTION

OF THE

UNITED STATES OF AMERICA.

We, the People of the United States, in order to form a more perfect Union, establish Justice, insure domestic Tranquility, provide for the common Defence, promote the general Welfare, and secure the Blessings of Liberty, to ourselves and our Posterity, do Ordain and Establish this Constitution for the United States of America.

ARTICLE I.

Of the Legislative power.

SECT. 1. ALL legislative powers, herein granted, shall be vested in a Congress of the United States, which shall consist of a Senate and House of Representatives.

SECT. 2. The House of Representatives shall be composed of members chosen every second year, by the people of the several states; and the electors in each state shall have the qualifications requisite for electors of the most numerous branch of the state legislature.

Of the House of Representatives.

No person shall be a Representative, who shall not have attained to the age of twenty-five years, and been seven years a citizen of the United States, and who shall not, when elected, be an inhabitant of that state in which he shall be chosen.

Representatives and direct taxes shall be apportioned among the several states which may be included within this union; according to their respective numbers, which shall be determined by adding to the whole number of free persons, including those bound to service for a term of years, and including Indians not taxed, three-fifths of all other persons. The actual enumeration shall be made within three years after the first meeting of the Congress of the United States, and within every subsequent term of ten years, in such manner as they shall by law direct. The number of Representatives shall not exceed one for every thirty thousand, but each state shall have at least one Representative; and until such enumeration shall be made, the state of New-Hampshire shall be entitled to choose three; Massacusetts, eight; Rhode-Island and Providence Plantations one; Connecticut, five; New-York, six; New-Jersey, four; Pennsylvania, eight; Delaware, one; Maryland, six; Virginia, ten; North-Carolina, five; South-Carolina, five; and Georgia, three.

When vacancies happen in the representation from any state, the executive authority thereof shall issue writs of election to fill such vacancies.

The House of Representatives shall choose their speaker and other officers; and shall have the sole power of impeachment.

Of the Senate.

SECT. 3. The Senate of the United States shall be composed of two senators from each state, chosen by the legislature thereof, for six years; and each senator shall have one vote.

Immediately after they shall be assembled in consequence of the first election, they shall be divided as equally as may be into three classes. The seats of the senators of the first class shall be vacated at the expiration of the second year, of the second class at the expiration of the fourth year, and of the third class at the expiration of the sixth year, so that one-third may be chosen every second year; and if vacancies happen by resignation, or otherwise, during the recess of the legislature of any state, the executive thereof may make temporary appointments until the next meeting of the legislature, which shall then fill such vacancies.

No person shall be a senator who shall not have attained to the age of thirty years, and been nine years a citizen of the United States, and who shall not when elected, be an inhabitant of that state for which he shall be chosen.

The Vice-President of the United States shall be President of the Senate, but shall have no vote unless they be equally divided.

The senate shall choose their other officers, and also a president *pro tempore*, in the absence of the vice-president, or when he shall exercise the office of President of the United States.

The senate shall have the sole power to try all impeachments. When sitting for that purpose, they shall be on oath or affirmation. When the President of the United States is tried, the Chief Justice shall preside: and no person shall be convicted without the concurrence of two-thirds of the members present.

Judgment in cases of impeachment shall not extend further than to removal from office, and disqualification to hold and enjoy any office of honor, trust or profit under the United States; but the party convicted shall nevertheless be liable and subject to indictment, trial, judgment, and punishment, according to law.

SECT. 4. The times, places, and manner of holding elections for senators and representatives, shall be prescribed in each state by the legislature thereof: But the congress may at any time by law make or alter such regulations, except as to the places of choosing senators. Manner of electing members:

The congress shall assemble at least once in every year, and such meeting shall be on the first Monday in December, unless they shall by law appoint a different day.

SECT. 5. Each house shall be the judge of the elections, returns and qualifications of its own members, and a majority of each shall constitute a quorum to do business, but a smaller number may adjourn from day to-day and may be authorised to compel the attendance of absent members, in such manner, and under such penalties as each house may provide. Powers of each house:

Each house may determine the rules of its proceedings, punish its members for disorderly behaviour, and, with the concurrence of two-thirds, expel a member.

Each house shall keep a journal of its proceedings, and from time to time publish the same, excepting such parts as may in their judgment require secrecy; and the yeas and nays of the members of either house, on any question, shall at the desire of one-fifth of those present, be entered on the journal.

Neither house, during the session of congress, shall without the consent of the other, adjourn for more than three days, nor to any other place than that in which the two houses shall be sitting.

Compensation, priviliges, and incapacities of the members.

SECT. 6. The senators and representatives shall receive a compensation for their services, to be ascertained by law, and paid out of the treasury of the United States. They shall in all cases, except treason, felony, and breach of the peace, be privileged from arrest during their attendance at the session of their respective houses, and in going to and returning from the same; and for any speech or debate in either house.

they shall not be questioned in any other place.

No senator or representative shall, during the time for which he was elected, be appointed to any civil office under the authority of the United States, which shall have been created, or the emoluments whereof shall have been increased during such time; and no person holding any office under the United States, shall be a member of either house, during his continuance in office.

SECT. 7. All bills for raising revenue shall originate in the house of representatives; but the senate may propose or concur with amendments as on other bills. Manner of passing bills, &c.

Every bill which shall have passed the house of representatives and the senate, shall, before it become a law, be presented to the President of the United States: if he approve, he shall sign it; but if not, he shall return it, with his objections, to that house in which it shall have originated, who shall enter the objections at large on their journal, and proceed to re-consider it. If after such re-consideration, two-thirds of that house shall agree to pass the bill, it shall be sent, together with the objections, to the other house, by which it shall likewise be re-considered, and if approved by two-thirds of that house, it shall become a law. But in all such cases, the votes of both houses shall be determined by yeas and nays; and the names of the persons voting for and against the bill, shall be entered on the journal of each house respectively. If any bill shall not be returned by the President within ten days (Sundays excepted) after it shall have been presented to him, the same shall be a law, in like manner as if he had signed it, unless the congress by their adjournment prevent its return, in which case it shall not be a law.

Every order, resolution or vote to which the concurrence of the senate and house of representatives may be necessary (except on a question of adjournment) shall be presented to the President of the United States; and before the same shall take effect, shall be approved by him, or being disapproved by him, shall be repassed by two-thirds of the senate and house of representatives, according to the rules and limitations prescribed in the case of a bill.

SECT. 8. The congress shall have power— Powers of Congress.

To lay and collect taxes, duties, imposts and excises, to pay the debts and provide for the common defence and general welfare of the United States; but all duties, imposts, and excises, shall be uniform throughout the United States.

To borrow money on the credit of the United States;

To regulate commerce with foreign nations, and among the several states, and with the Indian tribes;

To establish an uniform rule of naturalization, and uniform laws on the subject of bankruptcies throughout the United States;

To coin money, regulate the value thereof, and of foreign coin, and fix the standard of weights and measures;

To provide for the punishment of counterfeiting the securities and current coin of the United States;

To establish post-offices and post-roads;

To promote the progress of science and useful arts by securing for limited times to authors and inventors the exclusive right to their respective writings and discoveries;

To constitute tribunals inferior to the supreme court;

To define and punish piracies and felonies committed on the high seas; and offences against the law of nations;

To declare war, grant letters of marque and reprisal, and make rules concerning captures on land and water;

To raise and support armies; but no appropriation of money to that use shall be for a longer term than two years.

To provide and maintain a navy;

To make rules for the government and regulation of the land and naval forces;

To provide for calling forth the militia to execute the laws of the Union, suppress insurrections, and repel invasions;

To provide for organizing, arming, and disciplining the militia, and for governing such part of them as may be employed in the service of the United States, reserving to the states respectively, the appointment of the officers, and the authority of training the militia according to the discipline prescribed by congress;

To exercise exclusive legislation in all cases whatsoever, over such district (not exceeding ten miles square) as may by session of particular states, and the acceptance of congress, become the seat of the government of the United States, and to exercise like authority over all places, purchased by the consent of the legislature of the state in which the same shall be, for the erection of forts, magazines, arsenals, dock-yards, and other needful buildings; and

To make all laws which shall be necessary and proper for carrying into execution the foregoing powers, and all other powers vested by this constitution in the government of the United States, or in any department or officer thereof.

Limitations of the powers of Congress.

SECT. 9. The migration or importation of such persons as any of the states now existing shall think proper to admit, shall not be prohibited by the congress prior to the year one thousand eight hundred and eight; but a tax or duty may be imposed on such importation, not exceeding ten dollars for each person.

The privilege of the writ of *habeas corpus* shall not be suspended, unless when in cases of rebellion or invasion, the public safety may require it.

No bill of attainder or *ex post facto* law shall be passed

No capitation, or other direct tax shall be laid, unless in proportion to the *census* or enumeration herein before directed to be taken.

No tax or duty shall be laid on articles exported from any state. No preference shall be given by any regulation of commerce or revenue to the ports of one state over those of another: nor shall vessels bound to or from one state be obliged to enter, clear, or pay duties in another.

No money shall be drawn from the treasury but in consequence of appropriations made by law; and a regular statement and account of the receipts and expenditures of public money shall be published from time to time.

No title of nobility shall be granted by the United States: and no person holding any office of profit or trust under them, shall, without the consent of congress, accept of any present, emolument, office, or title of any kind whatever, from any king, prince, or foreign state.

Limitations of the powers of individual states.

SECT. 10. No state shall enter into any treaty, alliance or confederation, grant letters of marque and reprisal; coin money; emit bills of credit; make any thing but gold and silver coin a tender in payment of debts; pass any bill of attainder, *ex post facto* law, or law impairing the obligation of contracts, or grant any title of nobility.

No state shall, without the consent of the congress, lay any imposts or duties on imports or exports, except what may be absolutely necessary for executing its inspection laws; and the net produce of all duties and imposts, laid by any state on imports or exports, shall be for the use of the treasury of the United States; and all such laws shall be subject to the revision and control of the congress. No state shall, without the consent of congress, lay any duty of tonnage, keep troops, or ships of war in time of peace, enter into any agreement or compact with another state, or with a foreign power, or engage in war, unless actually invaded, or in such imminent danger as will not admit of delay.

ARTICLE II.

Of the Executive power.

SECT. 1. The executive power shall be vested in a President of the United States of America. He shall hold his office during the term of four years, and together with the Vice-President, chosen for the same term, be elected as follows:—

Manner of electing the President and Vice-President.

Each state shall appoint, in such manner as the legislature thereof may direct, a number of electors, equal to the whole number of senators and representatives to which the state may be entitled in the congress: but no senator or representative, or person holding an office of trust or profit under the United States, shall be appointed an elector.

The electors shall meet in their respective states, and vote by ballot for two persons, of whom one at least shall not be an inhabitant of the same state with themselves. And they shall make a list of all the persons voted for, and of the number of votes for each; which list they shall sign and certify, and transmit, sealed, to the seat of the government of the United States, directed to the President of the Senate. The president of the senate shall, in the presence of the senate and house of representatives, open all the certificates, and the votes shall then be counted. The person having the greatest number of votes shall be the President; if such number be a majority of the whole number of electors appointed; and if there be more than one who have such majority, and have an equal number of votes, then the house of representatives shall immediately choose by ballot one of them for President; and if no person have a majority, then from the five highest on the list the said house shall in like manner choose the President, but in choosing the President, the votes shall be taken by states, the representation from each state having one vote; a quorum for this purpose shall consist of a member or members from two thirds of the states, and a majority of all the states shall be necessary to a choice. In every case, after the choice of the President, the person having the greatest number of votes of the electors shall be the vice-president. But if there should remain two or more who have equal votes, the senate shall choose from them by ballot the vice-president.

The congress may determine the time of choosing the electors, and the day on which they shall give their votes; which day shall be the same throughout the United States.

Who may be elected President.

No person except a natural born citizen, or a citizen of the United States, at the time of the adoption of this Constitution, shall be eligible to the office of President—neither shall any person be eligible to that office who shall not have attained to the age of thirty-five years, and been fourteen years a resident within the United States.

In case of the removal, &c of the President, his powers to devolve on the Vice-President, &c.

In case of the removal of the President from office, or of his death, resignation, or inability to discharge the powers and duties of the said office, the same shall devolve on the vice-president; and the congress may by law provide for the case of removal, death, resignation, or inability, both of the President and vice-president, declaring what officer shall then act as President; and such officer shall act accordingly, until the disability be removed, or a President shall be elected.

President's compensation.

The President shall, at stated times receive for his services, a compensation, which shall neither be increased nor diminished during the period for which he shall have been elected; and he shall not receive within that period any other emolument from the United States, or any of them.

Before he enter on the execution of his office, he shall take the following oath or affirmation:

His oath.

"I do solemnly swear (or affirm) "that I will faithfully execute the office "of President of the United States; and "will, to the best of my ability, pre-"serve, protect, and defend the Consti-"tution of the United States."

Powers and duties of the President.

SECT. 2. The President shall be commander in chief of the army and navy of the United States, and of the militia of the several states, when called into the actual service of the United States; he may require the opinion, in writing, of the principal officer in each of the executive departments, upon any subject relating to the duties of their respective offices, and he shall have power to grant reprieves and pardons for offences against the United States, except in cases of impeachment.

He shall have power, by and with the advice and consent of the Senate, to make treaties, provided two-thirds of the senators present concur; and he shall nominate, and by and with the advice and consent of the senate, shall appoint ambassadors, other public ministers, and consuls, judges of the supreme court, and all other officers of the United States, whose appointments are not herein otherwise provided for, and which shall be established by law. But Congress may by law vest the appointment of such inferior officers, as they think proper, in the President alone, in the courts of law, or in the heads of departments.

The President shall have power to fill up all vacancies that may happen during the recess of the senate, by granting commissions which shall expire at the end of the next session.

Further powers and duties.

SECT. 3. He shall from time to time give to the Congress information of the state of the Union, and recommend to their consideration such measures as he shall judge necessary and expedient: He may on extraordinary occasions, convene both houses, or either of them; and in case of disagreement between them, with respect to the time of adjournment, he may adjourn them till such time as he shall think proper: He shall receive ambassadors and other public ministers: He shall take care that the laws be faithfully executed, and shall commission all the officers of the United States.

SECT. 4. The President, Vice-President, and all civil officers of the United States, shall be removed from office on impeachment for, an conviction of, treason, bribery, or other high crimes and misdemeanors.

How the President, &c. may be removed from office.

ARTICLE III.

SECT. 1. The judicial power of the United States, shall be vested in one supreme court, and in such inferior courts as the Congress may from time to time ordain and establish. The judges, both of the supreme and inferior courts, shall hold their offices during good behaviour; and shall, at stated times, receive for their services, a compensation, which shall not be diminished during their continuance in office.

Of the judicial power.

Concerning the Judges.

SECT. 2. The judicial power shall extend to all cases, in law and equity, arising under this Constitution, the laws of the United States, and treaties made, or which shall be made, under their authority; to all cases affecting ambas-

Extent of the judicial power.

sadors, other public ministers; and consuls; to all cases of admiralty and maratime jurisdiction; to controversies to which the United States shall be a party; to controversies between two or more states; between a state and citizens of another state; between citizens of different states; between citizens of the same state claiming lands under grants of different states: and between a state or the citizens thereof, and foreign states, citizens or subjects.

Of original and appellate jurisdiction of the supreme court.

In all cases affecting ambassadors, other public ministers and consuls, and those in which a state shall be a party, the supreme court shall have original jurisdiction. In all the other cases beforementioned, the supreme court shall have appellate jurisdiction both as to law and fact, with such exceptions, and under such regulations as the congress shall make.

Of trials for crimes.

The trial of all crimes, except in cases of impeachment, shall be by jury; and such trial shall be held in the state where the said crimes shall have been committed; but when not committed within any state, the trial shall be at such place or places as the congress may by law have directed.

SECT. 3. Treason against the United States, shall consist only in levying war against them, or in adhering to their enemies, giving them aid and comfort. No person shall be convicted of treason unless on the testimony of two witnesses to the same overt act, or on confession in open court. Of treason.

The congress shall have power to declare the punishment of treason; but no attainder of treason shall work corruption of blood or forfeiture, except during the life of the person attainted.

ARTICLE IV.

SECT. 1. Full faith and credit shall be given in each state to the public acts, records, and judicial proceedings of every other state. And the congress may by general laws prescribe the manner in which such acts, records, and Of records, &c.

proceedings shall be proved, and the effect thereof.

Of citizenship.

SECT. 2. The citizens of each state shall be entitled to all privileges and immunities of citizens in the several states.

Of fugitive criminals.

A person charged in any state with treason, felony, or other crime, who shall flee from justice, and be found in another state, shall, on demand of the executive authority of the state from which he fled, be delivered up, to be removed to the state having jurisdiction of the crime.

Of persons held to service.

No person held to service or labour in one state, under the laws thereof, escaping into another, shall, in consequence of any law or regulation therein, be discharged from such service or labour, but shall be delivered up, on claim of the party to whom such service or labour may be due.

Of new states.

SECT. 3. New states may be admitted by the congress into this Union; but no new state shall be formed or erected within the jurisdiction of any other state; nor any state be formed by the junction of two or more states, or parts of states, without the consent of the legislatures of the states concerned, as well as of the congress.

The congress shall have power to dispose of and make all needful rules and regulations, respecting the territory or other property belonging to the United States; and nothing in this constitution shall be so construed as to prejudice any claims of the United States, of any particular state.

Of the territory of the United States.

SECT. 4. The United States shall guarantee to every state in this Union, a republican form of government, and shall protect each of them against invasion; and on application of the legislature, or of the executive (when the legislature cannot be convened) against domestic violence.

Form of republican government guaranteed to the several states.

ARTICLE V.

The congress, whenever two-thirds of both houses shall deem it necessary,

Of amendments to the Constitution.

shall propose amendments to this constitution, or, on the application of the legislatures of two-thirds of the several states, shall call a convention for proposing amendments, which, in either case, shall be valid to all intents and purposes, as part of this constitution, when ratified by the legislatures of three-fourths of the several states, or by conventions in three-fourths thereof, as the one or the other mode of ratification may be proposed by the congress: Provided, that no amendment which may be made prior to the year one thousand eight hundred and eight, shall in any manner affect the first and fourth clauses in the ninth section of the first article; and that no state, without its consent, shall be deprived of its equal suffrage in the senate.

ARTICLE VI.

Of former debts.

All debts contracted and engagements entered into, before the adoption of this constitution, shall be as valid against the United States under this constitution, as under the confederation.

This constitution, and the laws of the United States, which shall be made in pursuance thereof; and all treaties made, or which shall be made, under the authority of the United States, shall be the supreme law of the land; and the judges in every state shall be bound thereby, any thing in the constitution or laws of any state to the contrary notwithstanding.

Force of the Constitution, laws, and treaties of the United States.

The senators and representatives before mentioned, and the members of the several state legislatures, and all executive and judicial officers, both of the United States, and of the several states, shall be bound by oath or affirmation, to support this constitution; but no religious test shall ever be required as a qualification to any office or public trust under the United States.

Of a political test.

Of a religious test.

ARTICLE VII.

The ratification of the conventions of nine states, shall be sufficient for the

Of the ratification of the constitution.

establishment of this constitution between the states so ratifying the same.

Done in Convention, by the unanimous consent of the states present, the seventeenth day of September, in the year of our Lord, one thousand seven hundred and eighty-seven, and of the independence of the United States of America, the twelfth. In witness whereof we have hereunto subscribed our names.

GEORGE WASHINGTON, *President,*
And Deputy from Virginia.

New-Hampshire.
John Langdon,
Nicholas Gilman.

Massachusetts.
Nathaniel Gorham,
Rufus King.

Connecticut.
William S. Johnson,
Roger Sherman.

New-York.
Alexander Hamilton.

New-Jersey.
William Livingston,
David Brearley,
William Paterson,
Jonathan Dayton.

Pennsylvania.
Benjamin Franklin,
Thomas Mifflin,
Robert Morris,
George Clymer,
Thomas Fitzsimons,
Jared Ingersoll,
James Wilson,
Gouverneur Morris.

Delaware.
George Read,
Gunning Bedford, jun.
John Dickinson,
Richard Bassett,
Jacob Broom.

Maryland.
James M'Henry,
Daniel of St. Thos. Jenifer.
Daniel Carrol.

Virginia.
John Blair,
James Madison, jun.

North-Carolina.
William Blount,
Richard Dobbs Spaight,
Hugh Williamson.

South-Carolina.
John Rutledge,
Charles C. Pinckney,
Charles Pinckney,
Pierce Butler.

Georgia.
William Few,
Abraham Baldwin.

Attest. WILLIAM JACKSON, *Secretary.*

IN CONVENTION,

Monday, September, 17, 1807.

RESOLVED, That the preceding constitution be laid before the United States, in congress assembled, and that it is the opinion of this convention, that it should afterwards be submitted to a convention of delegates, chosen in each state, by the people thereof, under the recommendation of its legislature, for their assent and ratification; and that each convention assenting to, and ratifying the same, should give notice thereof to the United States, in congress assembled.

RESOLVED, That it is the opinion of this convention, that as soon as the conventions of nine states shall have ratified this constitution, the United States in congress assembled, should fix a day, on which electors should be appointed by the states which shall have ratified the same, and a day on which the electors should assemble to vote for the President, and the time and place for commencing proceedings under this constitution; that after such publication, the electors should be appointed, and the senators and representatives elected. That the electors should meet on the day fixed for the election of the President, and should transmit their votes, certified, signed, sealed and directed, as the constitution requires, to the secretary of the United States, in congress assembled; that the senators and representatives should convene at the time and place assigned; that the senators should appoint a president of the senate, for the sole purpose of receiving, opening, and counting the votes for President; and, that after he shall be chosen, the congress, together with the president, should, without delay, proceed to execute this constitution.

By the unanimous order of the Convention,

GEORGE WASHINGTON, *President.*

WILLIAM JACKSON, *Secretary.*

IN CONVENTION,

September 17, 1787.

SIR,

WE have now the honor to submit to the consideration of the United States in congress assembled, that constitution which has appeared to us the most advisable.

The friends of our country have long seen and desired, that the power of making war, peace, and treaties, that of levying money, and regulating commerce, and the corresponding executive and judicial authorities, should be fully and effectually vested in the general government of the Union: but the impropriety of delegating such extensive trust to one body of men, is evident. Hence results the necessity of a different organization.

It is obviously impracticable, in the Federal Government of these states, to secure all rights of independent sovereignty to each, and yet provide for the interest and safety of all. Individuals entering into society must give up a share of liberty, to preserve the rest. The magnitude of the sacrifice must depend as well on situation and circumstance, as on the object to be obtained. It is at all times difficult to draw with precision the line between those rights which must be surrendered, and those which may be reserved; and on the present occasion, this difficulty was increased by a difference among the several states, as to their situation, extent, habits, and particular interests.

In all our deliberations on this subject, we kept steadily in our view that which appears to us the greatest interest of every true American, the consolidation of our union, in which is involved our prosperity, felicity, safety, perhaps our national existence. This important consideration, seriously and deeply impressed on our minds, led each state in the convention to be less rigid on points of inferior magnitude, than might have been otherwise expected; and thus the Constitution, which we now present, is the result of a spirit of amity, and of that mutual deference and concession, which the peculiarity of our political situation rendered indispensible.

That it will meet the full and entire approbation of every state is not, perhaps, to be expected; but each will doubtless consider, that, had her interest alone been consulted, the consequences might have been particularly disagreeable or injurious to others; that it is liable to as few exceptions as could reasonably have been expected, we hope and believe; that it may promote the lasting welfare of that country so dear to us all, and secure her freedom and happiness, is our most ardent wish.

With great respect,

We have the honor to be,

Sir,

Your Excellency's most obedient

And humble servants,

GEORGE WASHINGTON, *President.*

By the unanimous order of the Convention.

His Excellency the President of Congress.

THE UNITED STATES IN CONGRESS ASSEMBLED.

Friday, September 28th, 1787.

Present—New-Hampshire, Massachusetts, Connecticut, New-York, New-Jersey, Pennsylvania, Delaware, Virginia, North-Carolina, South-Carolina, and Georgia; and from Maryland, Mr. Ross.

Congress having received the report of the Convention lately assembled in Philadelphia.

Resolved unanimously,

THAT the said report, with the resolutions and letter accompanying the same, be transmitted to the several legislatures, in order to be submitted to a convention of Delegates, chosen in each state by the people thereof, in conformity to the resolves of the Convention, made and provided in that case.

CHARLES THOMPSON, *Secretary.*

CONGRESS OF THE UNITED STATES,

BEGUN AND HELD AT THE CITY OF NEW-YORK, ON WEDNESDAY, THE FOURTH OF MARCH, 1789.

The Convention of a number of the states having at the time of their adopting the Constitution expressed a desire, in order to prevent misconstruction, or abuse of its powers, that further declaratory and restrictive clauses should be added: And as extending the ground of public confidence in the government will best ensure the beneficent ends of its institution—

RESOLVED, by the Senate and House of Representatives of the United States of America, in Congress assembled, two-thirds of both Houses concurring, that the following Articles be proposed to the legislatures of the several states, as amendments to the Constitution of the United States, all or any of which Articles, when ratified by three-fourths of the said legislatures, to be valid, to all intents and purposes, as part of the said Constitution, viz.

ARTICLES, in addition to, and amendment of, the Constitution of the United States of America, proposed by Congress, and ratified by the legislatures of the several states pursuant to the fifth article of the original Constitution.

ARTICLE I.

Of representation.

AFTER the first enumeration required by the first article of the Constitution, there shall be one representative for every thirty thousand, until the number shall amount to one hundred; after which the proportion shall be so regulated by Congress, that there shall be not less than one hundred representatives, nor less than one representative for every forty thousand persons, until the number of representatives shall amount to two hundred; after which, the proportion shall be so regulated by Congress, that there shall not be less than two hundred representatives, nor more than one representative for every fifty thousand persons.

ARTICLE II.

No law varying the compensation for the services of the Senators and Representatives shall take effect, until an election of representatives shall have intervened.

Of the compensation of members of congress.

ARTICLE III.

Congress shall make no law respecting an establishment of religion, or prohibiting the free exercise thereof; or abridging the freedom of speech, or of the press; or the right of the people peaceably to assemble, and to petition the government for a redress of grievances.

Of the rights of conscience freedom of the press, &c.

ARTICLE IV.

Of the right to bear arms.

A well regulated militia being necessary to the security of a free state, the right of the people to keep and bear arms shall not be infringed.

ARTICLE V.

Of quartering troops.

No soldier shall in time of peace be quartered in any house, without the consent of the owner, nor in time of war, but in a manner to be prescribed by law.

ARTICLE VI.

Of the right to secure from searches, &c.

The right of the people to be secure in their persons, houses, papers, and effects, against unreasonable searches and seizures, shall not be violated; and no warrants shall issue, but upon probable cause supported by oath or affirmation, and particularly describing the place to be searched, and the persons or things to be seized.

ARTICLE VII.

No person shall be held to answer for a capital, or otherwise infamous crime, unless on a presentment or indictment of a grand jury, except in cases arising in the land or naval forces, or in the militia, when in actual service in time of war or public danger: Nor shall any person be subject, for the same offence, to be twice put in jeopardy of life or limb; nor shall be compelled, in any criminal case, to be a witness against himself; nor be deprived of life, liberty or property, without due process of law; nor shall private property be taken for public use, without just compensation.

Of indictments, punishments, &c.

ARTICLE VIII.

In all criminal prosecutions, the accused shall enjoy the right to a speedy and public trial, by an impartial jury of the state and district wherein the crime shall have been committed, which dis-

Of trial in criminal cases, and the rights of a defendant.

trict shall have been previously ascertained by law; and to be informed of the nature and cause of the accusation; to be confronted with the witnesses against him; to have compulsory process for obtaining witnesses in his favor, and to have the assistance of counsel for his defence.

ARTICLE IX.

Of trial in civil cases.

In suits at common law, where the value in controversy shall exceed twenty dollars, the right of trial by jury shall be preserved; and no fact tried by a jury shall be otherwise re-examined in any court of the United States, than according to the rules of the common law.

ARTICLE X.

Of bail, &c.

Excessive bail shall not be required, nor excessive fines imposed, nor cruel and unusual punishments inflicted.

ARTICLE XI.

Of rights reserved.

The enumeration in the Constitution of certain rights, shall not be construed to deny or disparage others retained by the people.

ARTICLE XII.

The powers not delegated to the United States by the Constitution, nor prohibited by it to the states, are reserved to the states respectively, or to the people. Of powers reserved.

FREDERICK A. MUHLENBERG,
Speaker of the House of Representatives.

JOHN ADAMS, *Vice-President of the United States, and President of the Senate.*

Attest.

JOHN BECKLEY, *Clerk of the House of Representatives.*
SAMUEL A. OTIS, *Secretary of the Senate.*

Note.—The ten last Articles of amendments have been adopted by three-fourths of the legislatures of the several states in the Union, and are become a part of the Constitution of the United States. The two first Articles have not been adopted.

Q q

THIRD CONGRESS OF THE UNITED STATES.

At the Second Session, begun and held at the city of Philadelphia, in the state of Pennsylvania, on Monday, the second of December, one thousand seven hundred and ninety-three.

RESOLVED, *by the Senate and House of Representatives of the United States of America, in Congress assembled, two-thirds of both Houses concurring,* That the following Article be proposed to the legislatures of the several states, as an amendment to the Constitution of the United States; which, when ratified by three-fourths of the said legislatures, shall be valid, as part of the said Constitution, viz.

The Judicial Power of the United States shall not be construed to extend to any suit in law or equity, commenced or prosecuted against one of the United States by citizens of another state, or by citizens or subjects of any foreign state.

FREDERICK A. MUHLENBERG,
Speaker of the House of Representatives.
JOHN ADAMS. *Vice-President of the United States, and President of the Senate.*

Attest.
JOHN BECKLEY, *Clerk of the House of Representatives.*
SAMUEL A. OTIS, *Secretary of the Senate.*

Note.—This Resolution was ratified by three-fourths of the States. See *Journals of Congress*, January 8th, and February 5th, 1798.

EIGHTH CONGRESS OF THE UNITED STATES.

At the First Session begun and held at the City of Washington, in the Territory of Columbia, on Monday, the seventeenth of October, one thousand eight hundred and three.

RESOLVED, *By the Senate and House of Representatives of the United States of America, in Congress assembled, two-thirds of both houses concurring,* That in lieu of the third paragraph of the first section of the second article of the Constitution of the United States, the following be proposed as an amendment to the Constitution of the United States, which when ratified by three-fourths of the legislatures of the several states, shall be valid to all intents and purposes, as part of the said constitution, to wit:—

The electors shall meet in their respective states, and vote by ballot for President and Vice-President, one of whom, at least, shall not be an inhabitant of the same state with themselves; they shall name in their ballots the person voted for as President, and in distinct ballots the person voted for as Vice-President; and they shall make distinct lists of all persons voted for as President, and of all persons voted for as Vice-President, and of the number of votes for each; which lists they shall sign and certify, and transmit sealed to the seat of government of the United States, directed to the President of the Senate; the president of the senate shall in the presence of the Senate and House of Representatives, open all the certificates, and the votes shall then be counted. The person having the greatest number of votes for President, shall be President, if such number be a majority of the whole number of electors appointed; and if no person have such majority, then from the persons having the highest numbers, not exceeding three, on the list of those voted for as President, the House of Representatives shall choose immediately, by ballot, the President. But in choosing the President, the votes shall be taken by states, the representation from each state having one vote; a quorum for this purpose shall consist of a member or members from two-thirds of the states, and a majority of all the states shall be necessary to a choice. And if the House of Representatives shall not choose a President, whenever the right of choice shall devolve upon them, before the fourth day of March next following, then the Vice-President shall act as President, as in the case of the death or other constitutional disability of the President.

The person having the greatest number of votes as Vice-President, shall be Vice-President, if such number be a majority of the whole number of electors appointed; and if no person have a majority, then from the two highest numbers on the list, the Senate shall choose the Vice-President; a quorum for the purpose shall consist of two-thirds of the whole number of Senators, and a majority of the whole number shall be necessary to a choice.

But no person constitutionally ineligible to the office of President, shall be eligible to that of Vice-President of the United States.

NATHANIEL MACON,
Speaker of the House of Representatives.
AARON BURR, *Vice-President of the United States, and President of the Senate.*

Attest,

JOHN BECKLEY, *Clerk of the House of Representatives.*
SAMUEL A. OTIS, *Secretary of the Senate.*

Note.—The above resolution was ratified by thirteen of the states, and has become a part of the Constitution of the United States.

INDEX.

A.

I.

J.

M.

INDEX TO THE APPENDIX.

A.

G.

J.

L.

M.

T.

W.

FINIS.

ERRATA

Page 25, line 7, from the bottom, for *requested,* read required.
70, 4, ditto, for *audable,* read audible.
71, 9, ditto, for *special,* read petit.
119, last line, for *farratry,* read barratry.
196, line 5, from the top, for *sentence,* read proceedings.